AND THE
SWASTIKA

Other books by F.T. Grossmith:

The Bottomless Pit - Calvary Evangelical Library
Dunkirk - a Miracle of Deliverance - Bachman and Turner

Cover Picture: Grand Admiral Raeder with
Hitler, Göring and von Blomberg

THE CROSS AND THE SWASTIKA

F. T. Grossmith

Pacific Press Publishing Association
Boise, Idaho
Oshawa, Ontario, Canada

THE CROSS AND THE SWASTIKA

Copyright © 1984 by F. T. Grossmith

This edition 1989 Pacific Press Publishing Association, Boise, Idaho, U.S.A. Co-published in association with Word (UK) Ltd.

First published by Henry Walter Ltd.

All rights reserved.

No part of this publication may be reproduced or transmitted in any form, electronic or mechanical, including photocopy, recording, or any information storage and retrieval system, without permission in writing from the publisher.

ISBN 0-8163-0837-3

Typesetting by Suripace Ltd, Milton Keynes.
Reproduced, printed and bound in Great Britain for Pacific Press Publishing Association by Cox and Wyman Ltd, Reading.

The Author with Albert Speer

FOREWORD

Henry Gerecke made a lasting impression on me. It was he who helped me through the trauma of the Nuremberg Trial. He was sincere and forthright. His outspokenness was not upsetting to us because everyone knew that he meant well. He was liked and appreciated by all the defendants.

Albert Speer
Adolf Hitler's Reich
Minister for Armaments
and War Production

ACKNOWLEDGEMENTS

This book is dedicated to those who proclaim the Gospel of our Lord Jesus Christ and I pray its story will prove an encouragement to all.

Without assistance the task could not have been completed and I wish to convey my sincere thanks and appreciation for the help given by: Dr. Aug. R. Suelflow of the Concordia Historical Institute, St. Louis; the editor of St. Louis Post-Dispatch; Saturday Evening Post; Lutheran Mission Association; Collins Memorial Library Washington; Missouri Historical Society; National Archives, Washington; Colonel Roger R. Venzke, U.S. Army; Colonel Vernon G. Swim, U.S. Army; Colonel Rd. R. Tupy, Commandant U.S. Army Chaplain Center and the late Albert Speer. I should like to thank Frau Margarete Speer for her kindness and hospitality plus those contemporary writers on the Nuremberg Trials whose skill with words helped me to sense the atmosphere and drama of an event which took place when I was very young. Last but not least, I wish to thank the surprising number of citizens of St. Louis who spared time to send me letters which proved instrumental in bringing to pass a book which I believe will gain a wide readership.

If unwittingly I have made some omission I trust any such oversight will be forgiven.

Frederick Grossmith.

CONTENTS

THE PATH TO THE GREATEST TRIAL IN HISTORY

1	A Tough Assignment	11
2	The Stage is Set	19

MEET THE CONGREGATION

3	The Policy Maker and the Reichsmarschall	29
4	A Soldier and Two Sailors	37
5	A Diplomat and an Agent of Misery	45
6	The Philosopher and the Nobleman	49
7	Two Bankers	53
8	Four Salesmen and Businessmen	57
9	The Congregation Gathers	61

THE CROSS AND THE SWASTIKA

10	Evil Omens	69
11	Stille Nacht	75
12	Darkness and Light	81

JUDGMENT

13	Judgment Day	95
14	Tussle with the Big Man	105
15	Tode Durch den Strang	113

EPILOGUE

16	The Man with a Warm Heart	121

THE PATH TO
THE GREATEST TRIAL IN HISTORY

How can a humble preacher, a one time farm boy, make any impression on disciples of Adolf Hitler?

Henry Gerecke

One

A Tough Assignment

V.E. Day - May 8th 1945 - and nearly six years of war with Nazi Germany was over. Hitler, the arch megalomaniac who saw himself as a man of destiny, was dead. The might and armour of the Third Reich - which, like an irresistible whirlwind of devastation, had overwhelmed Poland in seventeen days, Denmark in two, Norway in twenty four, Holland in five and Belgium in seventeen - lay crushed.

Mocking memories haunted German cities which had been ravaged by extensive air-attacks and the mechanised land power of the Allied forces: the hallowed soil from which was to emerge the 'Master Race' - a world-ruling breed such as never before witnessed by mankind - was now trodden down by the victorious Allied Armies. With the 'shooting' war over, the politicians deliberated the future of a suffering, conquered nation.

Long before V.E. Day, Allied leaders issued public pronouncements to the effect that after the war was won, those responsible for its outbreak, ensuing deprivation, suffering and atrocities, would be dealt with as 'War Criminals'. Three months after the termination of hostilities, August 8th 1945, Britain, America, France and Russia signed the London Agreement, giving birth to the International Military Tribunal. As early as 1943, Churchill, Roosevelt and Stalin had agreed that those responsible, by act or consent, for committing crimes against peace and for atrocities in occupied countries would be handed over to the Governments of those countries as soon as Hitler's Germany was squashed.

However, at the end of the war the four major powers, in an endeavour to illuminate the evils of the Nazi regime and its perpetrators, considered that the prevailing climate presented an opportunity to stage a public examination and exposure of leading Nazis against whom all the Allied Powers wished to bring charges - before a single court. This would then obviate the real possibility of these men's facing trial in twenty three different courts throughout the world, with varying kinds of justice and obvious complications, especially as the process could drag on for many years. Barely six months after Germany's capitulation, the list of those to be tried was published and the old city of Nuremberg, boasting a history dating back nearly one thousand years, was chosen.

For Chaplain Henry Gerecke - Major U.S. Army - the declaration that the war was over brought personal relief: his three sons had survived the war. At fifty two years of age, this Lutheran Minister from St Louis, Missouri, could look back upon nearly twenty years as a pastor since his graduation from St. Louis Seminary and ordination to the Christian ministry in January, 1926. Following fifteen months in England ministering to the sick and wounded, Gerecke arrived in Germany in June, 1945 assigned to the 98th General Hospital.

In November, 1945, his Commanding Officer, Colonel James Sullivan, summoned him into his office at their Munich headquarters. It was not an unusual request for his C.O. to make but what transpired in that room ushered the St Louis Pastor into turmoil. And dilemma!

A Tough Assignment 13

Captain Henry Gerecke

14 The Cross and The Swastika

Not far away, at Nuremberg, top Nazis close to Hitler were awaiting trial for War Crimes, and one of the accused, Gross Admiral Raeder, one-time Commander-in-chief of the German Navy until succeeded by Gross Admiral Dönitz, had asked his American jailor, Colonel Burton C Andres, Commander of Nuremberg Prison, for the services of a spiritual adviser.

An unexpected petition and the only one the Allies were willing to consider from those incarcerated in Nuremberg. Egotistical Hermann Göring, Chief of the Luftwaffe, had written a lengthy letter to American General Eisenhower, setting out many demands, and Churchill and other leaders were the recipients of similar letters from other defendants. The Allies were unbending, apart from offering to each of the accused the choice of his own defence lawyer with the promise of a fair trial.

Colonel Sullivan explained to Gerecke that he seemed the most suitable choice the army had around at the time. He spoke German, was Lutheran which the majority of the accused stated was their church - if only through being baptised as babies - and his records revealed considerable experience in prison visitation and counselling. Somewhat shaken and perplexed by the proposition, he searched his mind:

'How can a humble preacher, a one time farm boy, make any impression on disciples of Adolf Hitler?'

Sympathetically, Colonel Sullivan responded, informing the hesitant chaplain that the decision rested with him, but if he wanted a way out he could avail himself of the opportunity to transfer to the 'inactive' reserve which would inevitably lead to an immediate return to the United States. Gerecke needed time to be alone, time for his mixed emotions to settle, before giving his decision, a request which Colonel Sullivan understood and granted.

Over the next two days, Gerecke incessantly wrestled with questions to which he knew there was no answer. At one point he was prepared to take the way out suggested by Sullivan but lacked any peace of mind in such contemplation. Repeatedly, he asked himself how he could ever find a way to approach these evil men with the message of Jesus Christ and the Cross; how would they treat him?

The trial of the Germans was scheduled to commence on November 20th and a decision had to be made soon. But for the former Missouri farm boy the issue developed beyond the question of his ability or lack of it to undertake such a task. He had to search his heart. Although the U.S. Army would be satisfied that they were assigning an experienced man who spoke German fluently, it was not enough to Gerecke merely to be an instrument of compliance. There had to be a sense of calling! One question penetrated to the very core of his being, unrelenting, echoing down the very corridors of his soul, as he later wrote:

> How could I summon the right spirit worthy of
> a Christian which this mission demanded?

The question bore the disguise of a rude intruder but as he faced it this modern day Jacob, wearied in the pursuit of inward peace, longing for a refreshing dawn to sweep like an invisible hand across his troubled mind, arrived at the heart of the matter. Knowing the Scriptural teaching that without faith it is impossible to please God, he inwardly desired to be a real ambassador for his Lord:

> I had plenty of excuses for bitterness toward

them. I had been at Dachau Concentration Camp, where my hand, touching a wall, had been smeared with the human blood seeping through.

In England for fifteen months I had ministered to the wounded and dying from the front lines. My eldest son had been literally ripped apart in the fighting. The second suffered severely in the Battle of the Bulge.

Now faith gives a man the true prospect of things as they are. All our fears and discouragements arise from this, that men do not see things as they are. Henry Gerecke was a man of faith and prayer. During the short time granted him to reach a decision he prayed as never before, entering into deep agony of soul. From this emerged a man with a new mission:

Slowly, the men in Nuremberg became to me just lost souls, whom I was being asked to help if, as never before, I could hate the sin, but love the sinner.

On November 12th 1945, Chaplain Gerecke was assigned to the 6850th International Security Detachment, which had charge of the prisoners, and left for Nuremberg.

The city of Nuremberg was the hub of Nazism. Not to be outdone by the great rulers of the past, Hitler chose Nuremberg for the creation of a vast stadium to house his rallies, accompanied by massive pageantry and ceremony. The architectural genius of Albert Speer turned the 'Zeppelinwiese' into the principal parade ground for the 1930's rallies - an area of 835,000 square feet. Behind Hitler's grandstand, which itself towered 80 feet high, Speer illuminated the 170 white stone pillars with the use of 1200 spot lights. Hitler revelled in the splendour, turning the 1300 feet stretch into a huge pulpit from where he would captivate the mind and imagination of his hearers with stirring speeches, causing many to open their minds to his philosophy, committed to Hitler and his purposes to the exclusion of all else.

Around the stadium Speer planted 40,000 oak trees to add some green to the surroundings and, having a great love of flags, he delighted Hitler by flooding the 'Zeppelinweise' with spotlights to catch the banners and crowning eagles borne by parading groups who would enter the stadium under the veil of darkness to await the theatrical illumination of the spotlights. With Hitler's blessing, Speer went further by placing around the stadium 100 searchlights, to shine vertically, reaching a height of over 2,000 feet - the effect was dramatic.

Now the city from which it was often declared that the Third Reich would last a thousand years had become the centre of world attention, as Speer and his associates were accommodated under one roof for the trial of the century. But it was not by design the Allies chose Nuremberg - it was the only city with an undamaged court and prison large enough to cater for the hundreds of people who would be involved in the trial. When Gerecke arrived in Nuremberg there were no flags or splendour, but only evidence of the fierce battle for the city between the German First Army and the Americans. The acrid smell of defeat and destruction hung dismally in the air.

Two

The Stage is Set

The impetus to establish an international tribunal to try major war criminals was mooted by Allied leaders as early as 1941. The following year, The United Nations' War Crimes Commission was founded to acquire and compare information on war crimes and criminals. This enunciated no new policy, for the history of man records the practice of victors punishing those who had fought against them. Notwithstanding the absence of an international agreement defining the rules of war and the characteristics of a war criminal, there has always existed an interpretation of an unwritten code of ethics for the conduct of war - a kind of moral sensibility, determining what was acceptable or unacceptable.

All wars have resulted in specific charges against individuals who exceeded accepted rights, spreading misery through practices not reasonably related to the conduct of war. Accordingly, they were punished. In combat a soldier is expected, under orders, to kill or remove his enemy from the battle scene. Failure to obey renders him liable to military discipline. Alternatively, if he engages in killing his enemy after making him a prisoner-of-war or extends the process of undue suffering or liquidation against civilians in the occupied territory of a hostile nation, such actions are deemed criminal.

With the advent of the twentieth century, attention

was focused on these issues in a quest to develop a codification of the laws of war, with their embodiment, 'sine qua non', in international agreements. The Hague Conventions of 1907 set forth requirements for starting a war, emphasising the necessity to issue 'a reasoned declaration of war' or 'an ultimatum with conditional declaration of war'. The Geneva Prisoners of War and Red Cross Conventions of 1929 laid down rules for the treatment of prisoners and care of the sick and wounded. However, none of these treaties specified means of enforcing laws governing the conduct of war or consequential retribution for their violation. Nevertheless, many countries reshaped their military law, incorporating the new requirements.

Following the first World War, the Allied Powers drew up a list of forty five persons whom they considered guilty of breaking customary international law. Of these, twelve were tried by the German Government before the Supreme Court of Leipzig. German law was applied in weighing the charges and passing sentences but only six of the arraigned were convicted, leaving the Allied Powers' evaluation of justice somewhat dented.

In previous wars the indicted had appeared before the court of the country for war crimes committed against that country. Oftentimes, it was necessary for them to stand before several courts if their crimes affected more than one country. The crimes of the Nazi leaders the Allies wished to confront could not be identified with any particular country; in fact twenty three nations had gone to war with Germany at the price of an estimated thirty million deaths.

Inevitably, conflicting opinions on trial procedure ensued. Acting on behalf of the United Nations - representatives of the countries who had gone to war with Germany - Britain, France, the United States of America and the Soviet Union entered into negotiations on this matter. All were agreed that for the accused to appear before the courts of all the belligerent nations was not practicable. The agreement reached on August 8th, 1945 established the charter for an International Military Tribunal and the unprecedented decision of a group of victors to try war criminals together before the same court. As signatories to 'The London Agreement' of that date, the four major powers named twenty four Nazis and six organisations for indictment. There were four main counts on the indictment:

1. The crime of being party to a common plan or conspiracy to wage aggressive war (including the crimes of 2, 3 and 4).
2. Crimes against peace - planning, preparing, initiating or waging a war of aggression, or a war in violation of international treaties.
3. War Crimes - violation of the laws or customs of war, which included wanton destruction and the mistreatment of prisoners-of-war.
4. Crimes against humanity - inhuman treatment of civilians, extermination and persecution on racial or religious grounds.

A common indictment for twenty three nations was presented at Nuremberg, with the trial scheduled to commence on November 20th, 1945. The Tribunal was made up of four members: one judge from each Allied Power occupying Germany - Britain, France, the United States of America and the Soviet Union - with four judges in reserve.

In accordance with Article 16 of the Charter of the International Military Tribunal each defendant was served with his copy of the Indictment, a document of some 24,000 words, written in German and detailing in full the charges against him.

Each defendant was allowed the right to answer the charges and choose a lawyer to conduct his defence, with freedom to present evidence in his defence or cross-examine witnesses called by the Prosecution. The trial was to become the major topic of interest in the postwar world.

Situated one hundred miles north of Munich, Nuremberg, the city of Albrecht Dürer the fifteenth century painter, had fortifications dating from the Middle Ages. At one time the wealthiest and most important of the free imperial cities of the Bavarian Empire, it was singularly rich in medieval architecture. Its picturesque streets with their quaint gables and beautifully carved balconies had teemed with travellers. Tourist attractions included such favourites as the Gothic Church of St Sebaldus, rich in rare sculptures and paintings, the Rathhaus built in 1616 in the Italian Renaissance style containing a great hall adorned with frescoes by Dürer, and Dürer's house itself.

When the trial opened, Nuremberg was a scarred city, the rubble concealing 30,000 dead; the atmosphere plagued by the offensive smell of disinfectant. Beneath her ancient spires there was hardly a building undamaged.

The Palace of Justice on the western edge of the town had escaped serious damage. A solid municipal building connected to a prison, its courtroom could hold six hundred persons. There were also hundreds of offices for the lawyers and staff of the four prosecuting nations.

The Stage is Set 23

Nuremberg Court House 1946

At 10am on the appointed date for the trial, black robed judges (except for the Russian judges who chose to wear military uniforms) filed into their seats before the flags of the four nations. From that day until August 31st, 1946 the Tribunal sat five - sometimes five and a half - days a week, only allowing for short recesses over the accepted holiday periods. Judgment was delivered on September 30th and October 1st, 1946.

The defendants sat in two rows against one of the walls but three of the twenty four indicted did not stand trial. Dr Robert Ley, Reichsleiter and Chief of the German Labour Front, committed suicide by hanging himself in his cell. Gustav Krupp, the elderly head of German armaments, was dismissed from the proceedings on account of his senility. Martin Bormann, Hitler's deputy, was tried 'in absentia' as there was no proof he had died in Berlin as some reports had stated.

On the left of the defendants sat the judges; opposite at four tables the prosecution; and immediately in front three rows of benches accommodated their defence counsel. The trial was conducted in four languages simultaneously, and each seat in the court was fitted with headphones and a small selection switch so that whoever occupied the seat could listen to a translated version of what was said - in English, French, German and Russian. The service of the interpreters also extended to the press gallery occupied by up to two hundred journalists and photographers from every country in the world.

Outside the Palace of Justice the area came under the protection of American combat troops, always on the alert, never knowing if the persistent rumours of rescue bids on behalf of the prisoners -Nazi uprisings engineered by the SS - might be true. Five Sherman tanks guarded the courtroom with machine gun emplacements inside the courtyard. Inside the Palace of Justice the stage for the trial of the century was set, waiting for the spectacle of Germany's once mighty now powerless leaders standing trial for their lives. The gaze of the world was directed toward:

Hermann Göring	Reich Marshall and Commander-in-Chief of the Luftwaffe.
Rudolf Hess:	Deputy Führer until 1941.
Joachim von Ribbentrop:	Foreign Minister
Arthur Seyss-Inquart:	Governor of Austria and Reich Commissioner for Occupied Holland.
Alfred Rosenberg:	Reich Minister for the Occupied Eastern Territories.
Wilhelm Keitel:	Field-Marshal and Chief of the High Command of the Armed Forces. (O.K.W)
Karl Dönitz:	Grand Admiral, Commander in-Chief of the German Navy and Hitler's successor.
Erich Raeder:	Grand Admiral, Commander in-Chief of the German Navy 1928-43.
Ernest Kaltenbrunner:	Chief of the Security Police.
Hans Frank:	Governor-General of Poland.
Wilhelm Frick:	Reich Minister of the Interior and Reichs Protector of Bohemia-Moravia (occupied Czechoslovakia).
Julius Streicher:	Self styled 'Jew-baiter Number One'.
Albert Speer:	Reich Minister for Armaments and War

26 The Cross and The Swastika

Fritz Sauckel:	Production. Plenipotentiary General for the Allocation of Labour.
Hjalmar Schacht:	Reich Minister of Economics, 1935-37 and President of the Reichsbank until 1939.
Alfred Jodl:	Colonel-General, Chief of the Operations Section, High Command of the Armed Forces.
Walter Funk:	Reich Minister for the Economy and President of the Reichsbank.
Hans Fritzsche:	Head of Broadcasting Division in Propaganda Ministry.
Constantin von Neurath:	Foreign Minister 1932-38 and Reichs Protector of Bohemia-Moravia (occupied Czechoslovakia) 1939-41.
Baldur von Schirach:	Hitler Youth Leader and Gauleiter of Vienna.
Franz von Papen:	Former Chancellor and Special Envoy to Vienna.

MEET THE CONGREGATION

These men must be told about the Saviour bleeding, suffering and dying on the Cross for them.

Henry Gerecke

Three

The Policy Maker and The Reichsmarschall

Chaplain Henry Gerecke believed that Jesus Christ was sent into the world to save the human family from sin and its destructive results. The men to whom he would seek to present Christ were like all men without Christ - sinners. And sinners need pardon!

Eight days before the trial commenced Gerecke was met in Nuremberg by chaplain Carl Eggars, serving temporarily in the Protestant capacity, who briefed him as well as introducing his Roman Catholic counterpart - Chaplain Sixtus O'Connor. Ten years younger than Gerecke, the priest from New York spoke German well.

Assigned to Gerecke's care were Hess, von Ribbentrop, Rosenberg, Keitel, Dönitz, Raeder, Frick, Speer, Schacht, Funk, von Neurath, von Schirach, Sauckel, Göring and Fritzsche; and to O'Connor's care were Kaltenbrunner, Frank, von Papen, Streicher, Jodl and Seyss-Inquart.

The prisoners were confined in cells on the ground floor of the three storied prison block. Perhaps sensing the new arrival's reticence, Chaplain Eggars wasted no time in taking him to meet the 'congregation'. Gerecke admitted:

> I was terribly frightened. How could I say the right thing - and say it in German besides?

Eggars stopped first at the cell of Rudolf Hess, who had been held by the British authorities since 1941. Hess spoke English, so Eggars used it to introduce the newcomer:

'This is Chaplain Gerecke, who will be on duty here from now on. He will conduct services and be available for counsel if you wish to have him.'

The two men shook hands.

> I have been criticised for offering my hand to these men. Don't think it was easy for me. But I knew I could never win any of them to my way of thinking unless they liked me first. Furthermore, I was there as the representative of an all-loving Father. The gesture did not mean that I made light of their malefactions. They soon found that out!

Rudolf Hess was a strange man. Colonel Andrus the prison commandant and his staff watched him closely, hesitant in their deliberations concerning his mental health. Some believed he was mad - perhaps it was all an act? Nevertheless, the colonel was taking no chances. Already Dr Robert Ley, Chief of the German Labour Front, had strangled himself in the cell toilet, using the hem of a bath towel made into a noose. In February of that year, whilst in British custody, Hess had attempted suicide in Maindiff Court Hospital, near the town of Abergavenny in South Wales, stabbing himself in the chest with a breadknife.

Clothed in a greyish tweed coat which had known better days, without a collar and tie - one of Andrus's rules as a precaution against suicide attempts - Hess presented a dishevelled, pathetic appearance. On his feet

Hess with Hitler at a Nazi rally

were the flying boots he wore when parachuting 20,000 feet into Scotland. When captured he was wearing the uniform and insignia of a Luftwaffe captain, declaring he was on a special mission to the Duke of Hamilton. He said his name was Alfred Horn.

He had been a chivalrous character, serving during the First World War in the 16th Bavarian Regiment, the same regiment as Adolf Hitler, but it is not apparent that they met or knew each other at that time. After recovering from a chest wound he transferred to the German Air Force, becoming a pilot with the rank of Lieutenant.

Hess was urged to join the Nazi Party by Karl Haushofer, Professor of Geo-Politics at Munich University, who greatly influenced him in his student days. Hess was a Jew hater, taking part in numerous brawls and street violence. When the 'putsch' of 1923 failed he was sent to Landsberg Prison, where Hitler was already held.

Whereas a Christian holds the Holy Scriptures as the inspired Word of God, Hitler looked upon *Mein Kampf*, penned from his prison cell, as a repository of truth. If Hitler had been a praying man, he would have hailed Hess's arrival as an 'answer to prayer'. Hess formulated doctrines for German conquest, producing a generous response from Hitler. With some help from Alfred Rosenberg, a regular visitor to Landsberg, they produced a chronicle for Germany's redemption. *Mein Kampf* was destined to become the Nazi Bible - a library filled with ethnology, prophecy, political science and absolute rules for personal and social life. Hitler believed that ancient civilisations crumbled because the 'racial blood' was adulterated. Superior weapons did not necessarily indicate a superior nation: rather a nation's greatness depended upon the quality of its power to resist. Hitler intended all his prophecies to come true. Providence would write the sequel to *Mein Kampf* upon the pages of history, something like the Old Testament and the New Testament with Hitler playing the role of Messiah, creating a born-again Germany.

Released from prison, Hess was earnest in his support of Adolf Hitler, whom he venerated as a saviour from all the ills which beset his beloved Fatherland. Galloping inflation punctured the heart of a rapidly disintegrating nation, turning paper money into the mockery of the hour. In 1923 Hitler became Germany's new Chancellor, rewarding his faithful companion, who already shared his new religion of astrology, which relied on the illogical and irrational, with the post of Deputy Führer.

At forty nine years of age, with thick dark eyebrows, Hess was much younger than the majority of the defendants. Subject to bouts of amnesia, pale and worn-looking, this astrological slave collected horoscopes, allowing them seriously to programme his life. He was fearful that his keepers were trying to poison him. When Henry Gerecke stepped into his cell, the Deputy Führer was in a state of mental disarray.

'Would you care to attend chapel service Sunday evening?' Gerecke asked in German.

'No,' Hess replied bluntly - in English.

Gerecke tried again, this time speaking in English himself:

'Do you feel you can get along as well without attending, as if you did?'

'I expect to be extremely busy preparing my defence,' he retorted coldly. 'If I have any praying to do, I'll do it here.'

At this point Chaplain Eggars was called away, leaving a disconsolate counsellor:

> I knew I had accomplished nothing.

Carl Eggars did not return, and Gerecke had his own introductions to make:

> I stopped next at the cell of Hermann Göring. I dreaded meeting the big flamboyant egotist worse than any of the others.

Bavarian born Göring was fifty two years of age. During World War I he was rated amongst Germany's air aces, shooting down twenty two Allied aircraft and receiving his nation's highest recognition for gallantry. In 1916 he was shot down and badly wounded, but determination to get well again brought about a rapid recovery and twelve months later he was ready for

34 The Cross and The Swastika

further active service.

Like Hess he attended courses of political science at Munich University. In 1922 he met Hitler, who saw the political value of having a war hero in his camp. Vain and power-hungry, Hitler's new disciple rose to the head of the S.A. (Sturmabteilung) - brownshirted storm troops created to protect Nazi meetings. He indulged in ostentatious tailored uniforms befitting the ceremonial splendour he coveted. And titles! In 1932, he was elected President of the Reichstag. Soon he was Prussian Prime Minister, President of the Prussian State Council, Reich Minister of Aviation, Reich Forestry and Hunting Master, Chairman of the Ministerial Council for the Defence of the Reich and Commander-in-Chief of the Luftwaffe. He also founded the Gestapo and the first concentration camps.

Before entering the cell, Henry Gerecke motioned to the military policeman on guard duty to stand aside so that he could peer through the cell window, situated in the centre of the cell door at about shoulder height.

> Through the small aperture I had a chance to size him up for a moment. He was reading a book and smoking his meerschaum pipe.

When Gerecke entered the short, fat man, indefinably feminine and addicted to drugs, jumped up and clicked his heels. Gerecke greeted him in German, acknowledged by a respectful bow from the Reichsmarschall.

'Will you come in and spend some time with me?' he said with warmth. 'I heard you were coming and I am glad to see you.'

Willingly, Gerecke accepted the offer to occupy the

Reichsmarschall Hermann Göring

only chair in a sparsely furnished cell. Göring, his grey Air Force uniform tunic hanging loosely - he had gone down from twenty to fifteen stone since his imprisonment, being in much improved health - sat down upon his steel cot, fastened to the wall at one side of the cell door.

Göring was a rapid talker, asking the chaplain personal questions concerning his family. Not only did it seem too good to be true but for a moment it caused the surprised chaplain to ponder as to who was visiting whom.

> All my diffidence dissolved in his shrewdly calculated amiability.

Henry Gerecke left the cell feeling encouraged at his reception, uplifted by the promise Göring had given that his attendance at Sunday's chapel service could be counted on. Furthermore, Göring was concerned for Rudolf Hess:

> Then he asked if Hess had agreed to come. When I said no, he said he would speak to him about the matter.

Four

A Soldier and Two Sailors

Field Marshal Wilhelm Keitel, Chief of the German High Command, had been a serving officer for forty four years, continuing a long family tradition producing either military commanders or agricultural leaders. The son of a wealthy landowner, Prussian born and sixty two years of age, he had given unquestioned obedience to Adolf Hitler, whom he considered a military genius.

On May 10th, 1940, for the second time in twenty six years, Germany violated Belgium's neutrality, invading neighbouring Holland on the same day. To illustrate his genius, Hitler allowed his thrust into Belgium and Holland to bear the appearance of the famous Schlieffen Plan of 1914 with an enveloping sweep on the right flank. In 1914 the German Commander-in-Chief von Moltke, adhering to this plan, lost his nerve and refused to take in Holland in his drive to the west. German analysts have always declared it was a costly error which lost them the war. Hitler spared himself the same criticism by taking Holland into his calculations, confounding the Allies with a brilliantly conceived plan of deception. 'I succeeded,' he said, 'in deceiving the enemy staffs by inverting the Schlieffen Plan.'

The capitulation of Holland took five days - Belgium seventeen days. The French claimed that the Maginot Line, a vast bastion of steel and concrete stretching across the French -German border, could never be taken

Field Marshal Keitel

by frontal assault. Hitler was prepared to take them at their word. Instead, much to the dismay of his generals, he decided to attack through the Ardennes Forest, which the architects of the Maginot Line considered impassable. It was another surprise move, demonstrating to his generals German superiority. Thereafter they hailed their Führer 'Grosster Feldherr aller Zeiten' - the greatest general of all time.

Through the war Keitel was close to Hitler, involved in all major strategic decisions with responsibility for their conveyance to operational commanders. Unpopular amongst his military colleagues he collected several rather derisive nicknames: 'Nickesel', a toy donkey that nods its head, and 'La-Keitel' - a pun on the word 'lackey'. Commissioned into the artillery in 1901, he served as a battery officer during World War I, rising to the rank of Major General in 1934. Shortly before the outbreak of World War II he was serving as Chief-of-Staff to the Minister of War, and on Hitler's abolition of that office became head of the unified defence staff which was introduced to replace it. Typically Prussian in appearance and manner, and intelligent, it seemed reprehensible to him for a subordinate to question decisions of a Commander-in-Chief - a quality Hitler recognised and used to the fullest advantage. This earned him the nicknames from his fellow officers - and a place in the top list of Nazis drawn up by the Allied Powers.

Dressed in Field Marshal's tunic and breeches the grey headed old soldier, distinguished by a shortclipped moustache, welcomed the chaplain warmly. Still feeling like a door-to-door salesman on his first assignment, hesitant in anticipating the response each knock would bring, Gerecke was eager to impress.

'What are you reading?' he asked in an interested manner.

'My Bible,' said Keitel, softly. 'I know from this book that God can love a sinner like me.'

Keitel explained to his near speechless visitor, who had not been given even the slightest hint he would find any of the prisoners in possession of a copy of the Word of God, that he had carried it through both world wars.

> A phoney, I thought. But the longer I listened, the more I felt he might be sincere. He insisted he was very glad that a nation which would probably put him to death thought enough of his eternal welfare to provide him with spiritual guidance. He would be at chapel, he added.

Keitel knew his chances of surviving were very slim: he had signed the 'Commando Order' authorising, in accordance with Hitler's wishes, the execution of British commandos captured at Stavanger in 1942, despite the protests of General von Falkenhorst who tried to save their lives. Also, he was suspected of implication in the murder of fifty Royal Air Force officers recaptured following an escape from a prisoner-of-war camp in 1944.

'I was just getting ready for my daily devotions. Would you care to join me?' said Keitel reaching for his Bible.

> He knelt beside his cot and read a portion of Scripture. Then he folded his hands, looked heavenward and began to pray. Never have I heard a prayer quite like that one. He spoke penitently of his many sins and pleaded for mercy by reason of Christ's sacrifice for him.

In unison the two men said the Lord's Prayer. After pronouncing a benediction a strangely awed chaplain left the cell a different man from the one who had entered.

God was at work!

* * * *

The sight of Henry Gerecke walking into his cell aroused feelings of personal satisfaction and accomplishment within Erich Raeder. Due to his representations the Americans had acted quickly in sending a spiritual adviser with the express purpose of ministering to him and his colleagues for the duration of the trial. It was therefore to be expected that he would agree readily to accept the chaplain's invitation to Sunday's chapel service.

A quiet, fussy man, he sold Hitler the idea of building a strong navy, placing a special emphasis on the pocket battle-ship. Proud of his physical fitness, Raeder was sixty nine years of age. His naval career traced its beginnings to 1894 when he enlisted as a cadet. During World War I he commanded a light cruiser and was promoted admiral in 1928. Seven years later he was Commander-in-Chief of the German Navy, reaching the ultimate in 1939 - Grand Admiral. Under provocation he was not afraid to argue with Hitler over the value and usefulness of his particular pride - the pocket battleship. However, his failure to check Allied successes in sending convoys to Russia singled him out for the full wrath of his infuriated Führer. In 1943 Hitler accepted his resignation, replacing him with Admiral Dönitz, the U-boat supremo. But he held no grudge towards his successor.

'Be sure to visit my friend Admiral Dönitz,' urged Raeder, as Gerecke prepared to leave his company, satisfied that a good foundation had been laid to build upon in future visits.

* * * *

Grand Admiral Karl Dönitz, Commander-in-Chief of Germany's Navy and Hitler's choice to follow him as Chancellor of the Third Reich, argued with Gerecke, insisting he could hardly preach the Gospel without bringing in politics.

Once the chief of the world's mightiest submarine fleet, he became leader of Nazi Germany on April 30th, 1945 and for twenty three days he held power, supervising the surrender of German forces to the Allies who dissolved his brief government on May 23rd.

Aged fifty four and born in Berlin, he joined the navy in 1910 as a cadet, becoming an officer in 1913. Whilst attacking a British convoy the submarine he commanded, U-68, sustained a direct hit. A British destroyer rescued Dönitz from the sea and he spent the remainder of the First World War in a prison camp. At the close of hostilities he continued his career and in 1935, whilst captain of the cruiser *Emden*, he was promoted to Commander of the U-boat arm.

A brilliant seaman, Hitler saw in Dönitz also a man of vision sensitive to the possibility of war. His dream was to build a large submarine fleet capable of penetrating the Atlantic Ocean and remaining at sea for long periods of time. Ignoring the miscalculations of others he declared that 300 operational boats would give German mastery of the seas. Had he been given full co-operation, the Battle of the Atlantic might have been recorded quite differently. But war came six years too early. In 1943 he succeeded Raeder as Commander-in-Chief of the German Navy combining the post with Commander of the U-boat fleet.

Gerecke determined to face up to the Admiral and last Chancellor of the Third Reich:

> I assured him that I knew little about politics, and, since he would not be interested in mine, we would simply deal with the Word of God in relation to the hearts of men.

Karl Dönitz knew the loneliness of command. And he had the gift of summing up character. He said:
'If you have the courage to come here, I'll attend your

services. I think you'll probably help me.'

God's servant was growing in stature and in the power of the Holy Spirit.

Grand Admiral Karl Dönitz

Five

A Diplomat and an Agent of Misery

Arrogant and snobbish, Foreign Minister Joachim von Ribbentrop made no attempt to conceal his cool indifference at the sight of the chaplain entering his untidy cell.

An unfriendly man, disliked by his colleagues, he was fifty two years of age but looked older. Educated in Alsace, Switzerland and London he then emigrated to Canada, working in a variety of employments. In 1914 he returned to Germany, earning a commission in the 12th Hussars, and was wounded during the bitter fighting over those four months of war. For his gallantry Lieutenant Ribbentrop was decorated with the Iron Cross.

In the 1920's he was in business as the overseas representative of a wine merchant, an experience which later took the attention of Hitler who was impressed by his knowledge of foreign countries, languages and important persons. In 1933, a year after joining the Nazi Party, Hitler appointed him as his personal adviser on foreign affairs. In 1936 he was appointed Ambassador to London and two years later Germany's Foreign Minister. A student of dramatic art, he exhibited theatrical reactions, much to the disdain of professional German diplomats who viewed him as a tactless man with no pedigree. Diplomatic relations with Britain suffered a severe strain when he greeted King George VI with a

46 The Cross and The Swastika

Foreign Minister von Ribbentrop

'Heil Hitler' salute.

Strongly anti-semitic, he considered the Jews a useless breed of people, disfiguring their stay on earth by thieving and murderous intents.

Hjalmar Schacht, Hitler's economic wizard, openly criticised Ribbentrop, calling him 'vain and incompetent'. He told Dr Gilbert, Nuremberg's Prison Psychologist, that 'he should be hanged for his stupidity'. In order to rejuvenate his drooping influence, rapidly eroded in the closing years of the war, the former champagne salesman appeared to be highly delighted that the Allies had chosen to arrest and interrogate him, insisting throughout that he was a very important person. Gerecke felt awkward in the presence of this unpopular man who would offer no promise to attend Sunday's chapel service, commenting, 'This business of religion isn't so serious as you consider it'.

Gerecke took his leave, promising to call again. This was a hard man to love!

A Diplomat and an Agent of Misery 47

To visit a man described as 'the greatest and cruellest slaver since the Pharaohs of Egypt' is disconcerting, to say the least. Such was the description given to Fritz Sauckel by Justice Robert Jackson.

Fifty two years of age and the son of a postman, the Nazi chief of slave recruitment was the father of eleven children. As a cabin boy he went to sea, sailing the world in clipper ships only to be interned by the French at the beginning of World War I. Five years later he returned to Germany, taking up employment as a factory hand in Schweinfurt where he rose to be a labour leader, participating in many strikes and labour negotiations. In 1939 Hitler appointed him Reichsleiter of Thuringia, and a general in both the Schutzstaffel (the SS) and the Sturmabteiling (the SA).

However, his importance dates from his appointment as Plenipotentiary General for the Allocation of Labour in 1942. As chief labour organiser under Albert Speer he received mandatory powers to instigate the mobilisation of German and foreign workers, including prisoners of war in the Reich and occupied countries. Over the next three years he was responsible for the deportation of some eight million people from their homes to Germany. Documentary evidence proves that he wanted the deportees treated well but at the minimum of financial expenditure, at the same time exploiting them to the highest possible extent. Although he persistently propagated the necessity for humane treatment of the slaves, he had no authority to change the disgusting conditions prevailing in many labour camps. Neither did he raise his voice in objection to these deprivations.

The chaplain was confronted by an obviously frightened man, a great contrast to Ribbentrop. A 'rough and ready' character, Sauckel eagerly gripped the chaplain's hand, shaking it almost emotionally as if a

48 The Cross and The Swastika

long-lost friend had suddenly come back into his life:

> He put his hands on my arms and said with great feeling, 'As a clergyman, you are one person to whom I can open my heart.' During our conversation he would wipe away tears and speak earnestly of his faithful wife and eleven children, one of whom had been killed in the war.

Gerecke left Cell 11 with the conviction that here was a soul who really needed him.

Fritz Sauckel

Six

The Philosopher and the Nobleman

The *Myth of the Twentieth Century* sold over one million copies and was considered by many as the principal statement of Nazi ideology. It was also a book through which its author Alfred Rosenberg launched a bitter attack on Christianity.

Born in the German community of Revel, Estonia - then part of Russia - the fifty two year old Nazi philosopher, educated as an architect in Moscow, left his homeland after the 1917 Revolution, joining the Nazi Party in 1919. He was later appointed by Hitler as Reich Minister for the occupied Eastern Territories. During Hitler's time in Landsberg prison he was a regular visitor, and there is no doubt that *Mein Kampf* is permeated with his philosophies. He hated everything Bolshevic and Russian, attributing Russia's troubles to the outcome of a sinister Jewish-Zionist plot.

To Rosenberg National Socialism, with its doctrine of racial purity, was the true gospel and he saw a new religion emerging out of the inner nature of Aryan man once he was liberated from adulterous blood-mixing. These views were projected in the Party newspaper *Volkischer Beobachter* which he edited. His books attacking Jewry and Bolshevism influenced Hitler, in particular the evidence he presented of a Jewish conspiracy for world domination.

Rosenberg held a pantheistic view of God, a belief

Alfred Rosenberg

deduced through a study of writings made by thirteenth and fourteenth century mystics. He rejected the Christian Gospel proclaiming Jesus Christ as the Way of Salvation. In his mind Jesus was a Jew, and Christianity as set forth in the New Testament was tarnished by Jewish elements introduced by its writers.

The tall slender philosopher greeted Henry Gerecke with forced politeness:

> He told me that he felt no need of my help. I would be welcome if I cared to visit - but perhaps I had better spend the time with his colleagues.

The Philosopher and the Nobleman 51

Constantin von Neurath came from the nobility of Württemberg and had grown up surrounded by the splendour of his parents' estate. As a young man he joined the German Foreign Service becoming a member of the London Consular Staff. Wounds received in the First World War cut short any prospect of a military career but not before he honoured the family tradition with gallantry and an Iron Cross, First Class.

Baron von Neurath

Resuming his diplomatic service he acted as head of the King of Württemberg's Cabinet until 1918. There then followed a series of overseas postings, each developing his diplomatic status: Minister to Denmark, 1919-21; Ambassador to Italy, 1921-30; Ambassador to Great Britain, 1930-32, reaching distinction in 1932 when he was appointed Germany's Foreign Minister, an office he held until 1938.

In disapproval of Hitler's plans for aggressive war he resigned, to be succeeded by von Ribbentrop. Nevertheless, Hitler wanted to retain the services of a highly regarded member of his Foreign Service, offering him the position of Governor of occupied Czechoslovakia in 1939. But it did not last for long. Mounting pressure from Hitler to be more harsh towards the Czechs, an order he had no intention of fulfilling, left him with little alternative but to tender his resignation.

At seventy three the cultured, well-mannered old baron had received or been received by countless representatives of governments, but Henry Gerecke represented an area of life that had held little interest at any time in his long career. To be invited in his autumn years to a church service was novel, causing an awkward silence. Gerecke left the cell promising to return.

Seven

Two Bankers

Undoubtedly the most surprised, if not annoyed, client on the chaplain's list was Hjalmar Schacht. Since 1939 he had held no office, living privately until 1944 when he was arrested and sent to Flossenberg Concentration Camp under suspicion of conspiracy in the bomb plot on Hitler's life. Freed by the Americans in 1945 he expected treatment worthy of a hero: instead of honouring him the liberators listed him as a war criminal.

At sixty nine, tall and thin, Schacht proved the most intelligent of the group awaiting trial. His whole career had been in finance, revealing a dedicated man committed to making money, amassing a personal fortune before he had reached middle age. During World War I he served as economic director of occupied Belgium, and was appointed Currency Commissioner in 1923, with the unenviable task of halting the high inflation caused by the war. Successfully he stabilised the German currency, earning the presidency of the Reichsbank in 1924, and recognition as a key figure in developing German economic recovery. In 1935 Hitler handed him the job of Economics Minister. He reorganised the German financial system, dealing skilfully in the money market. His genius aided the Nazi Party in financing the early stage of German rearmament. But Schacht's ambition was to build a better

Fatherland and he did not take kindly to Göring's assuming control of the German economy.

At variance with Nazi economic policy and ideology, he resigned his Ministry in 1937. Further disagreements with Hitler over basic policies, in particular the frenzied concentration on armaments which Schacht felt would unsettle economic advances, reached a climax in 1939 and Hitler removed him as President of the Reichsbank.

A man of phlegmatic temperament awaited Gerecke's visit, ruled more by his intellect than by his heart. Solely interested in contesting the 'unjustified' indictment he had to face, he treated Gerecke in a legalistic, business-like manner. He coldly advised his caller that he had never left the Lutheran Church and if a Lutheran minister was holding chapel services then he would be there. As Gerecke left to call upon Walter Funk he realised a most unusual congregation was taking shape - perhaps the most unusual any pastor could claim to have gathered.

* * * *

Walter Emmanual Funk was a short, fat man of fifty five years. Invalided from the army in 1916, he worked as a journalist on several Berlin papers. In 1922 he was employed as editor of the *Berliner Borsenzeitung*, a financial paper, but resigned his editorship in 1931 to join the Nazi Party. Sensing the Party would soon be in power, he was keen to make his own political and economic opinions heard. In January 1933 Hitler made him party press chief, elevating him two months later into the office of State Secretary in the Ministry of Propaganda. In 1937 he succeeded Schacht as Reich Minister for the Economy and in 1939, as President of the Reichsbank.

He was in a different league from Schacht, of only average intelligence, impressionable and unsure of himself. However, the Allies thought that the man who hoarded in the Reichsbank vaults gold teeth and fillings extracted from the mouths of the regime's millions of victims was sufficiently important to be labelled a 'war criminal'.

Full of self-pity, Funk is reputed to have made more complaints about prison conditions than any other defendant. Like Hess, he believed in astrology. Henry Gerecke found him a difficult man to communicate with.

Hjalmar Schacht   *Walter Funk*

Eight

Four Salesmen and Businessmen

Every manufacturer needs a sales outlet and Dr Josef Goebbels, Hitler's Minister of Propaganda, set up a salesforce to market Nazi doctrine.

Hans Fritzsche was chief of the Radio Section of Goebbels' Propaganda Ministry and well-known as a broadcaster. Born in 1900 in Westphalia, the son of a civil servant, he attended Berlin University where he studied history and political economy. Afterwards he took up journalism and through his work as a writer met Goebbels, whom he impressed. Frtizsche was a Jew hater, and his broadcasts proved a continuous commercial for the Nazi Party, propagating high sounding expressions deifying German superiority, persuading the people to get their priorities into true perspective by making the interests of the German State paramount, and placing implicit trust in Adolf Hitler. It appealed to Fritzsche's journalistic mind to attend church and hear what the short, stocky, smiling chaplain had to offer.

* * * *

Hitler campaigned to win the allegiance of Germany's youth. The organisation set up to indoctrinate young people with Nazi ideology was capably led by chief salesman Baldur von Schirach, an aristocrat who became

58 The Cross and The Swastika

Gauleiter of Vienna. He had manifested a fanatical enthusiasm for Hitler and the youth programme. By 1936 all German youth organisations, including religious orientated movements and the Boy Scouts, were under his control. At thirty-eight he was the youngest defendant, and Gerecke found his boyish smile disarming but detected a genuineness in von Schirach's desire for frequent visits.

Hans Fritzsche *Baldur von Schirach*

* * * *

It was hard to realise that the friendly almost mild-mannered man who was shaking Gerecke's hand was a ruthless killer. During his term as Protector of Bohemia-Moravia (occupied Czechoslovakia) Wilhelm Frick acquiesced willingly in a reign of terror and extermination. Hitler regarded him highly, valuing his administrative expertise. Frick obtained his law degree and his doctorate from Munich University. Since its inception, the Nazi Party had held an attraction for him, and he had used his position as Deputy Chief of the Munich Police to Hitler's advantage, saving him from arrest. Trade Unions were outlawed due to the new legislation brought about at his instigation. His responsibility for the anti-semitic Nuremberg Laws aimed at German racial purity had also resulted in Jewish persecution.

His short-cropped hairstyle gave him the appearance of coming from old Prussian military stock. But there the resemblance stopped - he was a Nazi without conscience toward the terrible human suffering he had caused. Gerecke was in no doubt that Frick would never live to celebrate his seventieth birthday. He had but a limited time to work and pray for the salvation of this unemotional soul.

* * * *

Leaving Albert Speer's cell, Gerecke completed his day's visiting on a positive note, recording alongside the name of Hitler's former architect a definite response for Sunday's chapel service. Hailed as the greatest manager Europe had known, Speer possessed remarkable powers of organisation. Until the end Hitler respected him more than any of his other Ministers.

Joining the Nazi Party in 1932 he became Hitler's personal architect and notable among the commissions he received were those for the new Reich Chancellory at Berlin and the Party Palace at Nuremberg. From 1942 until hostilities ended he was Reich Minister of Armaments and War Production as well as head of the Todt Organisation which undertook state construction work. Despite massive air attacks on German industry

60 The Cross and The Swastika

Speer was able to increase production of essential materials throughout 1943 and most of 1944.

In the last months of the war he schemed to kill Hitler, boldly defying his orders to raze Germany's industry to the ground. Speer was honest with Hitler, who imposed no punishment upon him for his act of disobedience. Other colleagues had been shot for lesser offences, but Speer walked free. It was the last time he saw the Führer, who excited him with visions of buildings he would design for 'the thousand year Reich'.

His success as labour and construction chief could never have been accomplished without the efforts of his aide Fritz Sauckel, who, as already mentioned, mobilised a slave labour force of eight million people. For this reason Speer stood indicted.

Wilhelm Frick   *Albert Speer*

Nine

The Congregation Gathers

Special times have demanded special men. Some have lived in controversial periods of history; they have been equipped for controversy, strong in argument and defiant in spirit, intrepid and courageous. Others have faced suffering, deprivations, persecutions, discovering the power of endurance as a weapon of victory. Briefly, they appeared upon mankind's stage but today their meritorious deeds, deeply and divinely felt, their words spoken in a just cause, their fight against wicked practices and defence of moral landmarks, live on.

That night as he thought about the men he had visited and the task at hand, Henry Gerecke knew he had some decisions to make. Above all else he desired to be a true pastor to these unloving and unlovely prisoners whose collective crimes were a dark blot upon God's earth.

As never before he felt his need:

> That night I had to have a little talk with Jesus, asking Him to do something especially for me. I felt a great need of just what I knew God could give me. Yet from that moment on I decided to love the sinner and to hate his sins. I recalled too, that God loves sinners. These men must be told about the Saviour bleeding, suffering and dying on the Cross for them.

As Sunday 18th November approached, Chaplain Henry Gerecke was untiring in his visitation. He was a man with a mission! Once the prophet Isaiah said: 'The Lord God will help me'. Gerecke knew that victory lay not in the fighter but in the spirit of the fighter. He had a battle on his hands for the salvation of 'Hitler's gang' and whatever he did must be done in the spirit of Christ and for the sake of Christ.

Once Jesus shared with His disciples His curiosity regarding public opinion over His identity. Then He made it very personal by asking them who *they* thought He was. Jesus rejoiced at Simon Peter's clear affirmation, assuring him that knowing who Christ is can only come by Divine revelation.

As a Lutheran, Gerecke believed that the Bible was 'given by inspiration of God' and, according to Luther's Catechism, for the purpose of making us 'wise unto salvation through faith which is in Jesus Christ'. When Gerecke opened his Bible to the accused, be believed it was the living Word of God bringing a revelation of God's rescue mission to lost and sinful man. Luther's Catechism further declares:

> I believe that I cannot by my own
> strength believe in Jesus Christ my Lord
> or come to Him; but the Holy Ghost has
> called me by the Gospel, enlightened me
> with His gifts, sanctified and kept me in
> the true faith.

Gerecke believed that there was a heaven to gain and a hell to shun, that man was not merely superficially inflicted by sin, but his whole nature was total corruption. He knew that man's only hope was in confession and repentance, for 'the blood of Jesus Christ cleanseth from all sin'.

In answer to prayer, some of the doubtful ones seemed more responsive. Joachim von Ribbentrop asked, with a troubled frown:

'Can a man be patriotic and Christian at the same time?'

The question afforded Gerecke an opportunity to do what he was best at - sharing the Scriptures with a needy soul. A beginning had been made as he persuaded the Foreign Minister to read Romans chapter 13 verse 1:

> Let every soul be subject unto the higher powers. For there is no power but of God: the powers that be are ordained of God.

He went on to verse 7:

> Render therefore to all their dues: tribute to whom tribute is due; custom to whom custom; fear to whom fear; honour to whom honour.

'Of course you can be patriotic and Christian too provided you do according to Romans,' Gerecke went on, 'until you come into conflict with Acts chapter 5 verse 29. This is where Peter and the other apostles told the council, "We ought to obey God rather than men".'

Ribbentrop wasn't convinced, as Gerecke discovered in future visits. It was a question which disturbed his peace. But he did promise to attend Sunday's chapel service.

An unexpected but welcome gesture came from

Albert Speer who during exercise periods was overheard urging other to be at the service. Göring kept his promise to speak to Hess about attending chapel:

> He and Hess were conducted to the exercise yard for the same quarter of an hour. Though they were forbidden to communicate, I distinctly overheard Göring get across to Hess that it would doubtless be in their favour to appear at chapel. 'I wouldn't give it a thought,' Hess retorted. The next time I saw Göring, he apologised for his failure to persuade his colleague. A wily fellow, Hermann Göring.

Declining the chaplain's offer of prayer Alfred Rosenberg, like Hess, refused to accept a copy of John's Gospel, mockingly saying, as Gerecke recalls:

> He thought it was nice if anyone could be so simple as to accept the story of the Cross as I told it.

Since the regular prison chapel had been set aside for the use of several hundred witnesses confined to the prison, Colonel Andrus helped Gerecke over the problem by providing a tiny improvised chapel composed of two cells with the wall knocked out. Its only furniture was a small altar, organ and chairs for the congregation.

Göring told Dr Gilbert, the prison psychologist, that he only went to chapel in order to be away from his cell. Nevertheless, from whatever motive the prisoners came, it was a heartening sight for the chaplain as they took their places:

> Göring stumped into the little chapel first in order to get a seat at the front. When singing, no one boomed louder than Göring, almost drowning the organ.

At the organ sat a trial witness Walter Schellenberg, a lieutenant-colonel in the SS. As an act of faith fifteen chairs were put out and Gerecke was well pleased to see thirteen of the men under his pastoral care awaiting the commencement of the service. The only absentees were Hess and Rosenberg, which saddened him. However, two unexpected visitors, Hess's secretary and Field Marshal Kesselring, both trial witnesses, filled the vacant seats.

That night Gerecke wrote to his wife Alma in St Louis:

> Another day with the men upon whom all the world has set its eyes, and most for condemnation. Well maybe so, but there's something going on inside their hearts since I have been seeing them that can only be measured in spiritual value.
>
> I preached the first German sermon in fifteen years and it wasn't too easy. Yet I got through it in good style according to the high-ranking Nazi witnesses. They said that they were truly moved by the way I presented the Gospel to them.
>
> I hope they were not kidding, because some of them will need everything God can give them to meet their end. The

> little place was packed and a preacher's son led the singing for me. Hess's former secretary was in the service. She claims it's the first one she's attended since the Party got in to power.
>
> They were all confirmed Lutherans. Kesselring was moved to tears in the sermon. He is one gentleman who stands out above the lot, I think.

Following the close of the service, Fritz Sauckel expressed a wish to talk with Gerecke. Later that day the chaplain visited his cell. At first Sauckel just wanted to talk about his good wife and faithful children, asking questions about Gerecke's wife and family, which the chaplain readily answered. Sensing there was more he wished to speak of, he brought their conversation around to spiritual affairs. Suddenly, Sauckel knelt down by his bed imploring Gerecke to read the Scriptures and pray with him:

> Unafraid and unashamed he prayed with me at his bedside, generously ending our prayer by saying, 'God be merciful to me, a sinner'.

With brokenness Sauckel arose from his knees and Gerecke's heart rejoiced at this early breakthrough in his ministry. Jesus said:

> Likewise, I say unto you, there is joy in the presence of the angels of God over one sinner that repenteth.

The Cross and the Swastika

Yes, I believe it; I am a sinner.

Fritz Sauckel

Ten

Evil Omens

Easily identifiable by the masses, Hitler's Swastika symbolised National Socialism, its ideals and struggles. The striking design of a black Swastika on a white disc with a red background was credited to Dr. Friedrich Krohn, a dentist. And an occultist.

Before the twentieth century the Swastika was known as the Fylfot Cross, or the Hammer of Thor. In mythology Thor was the strongest of the gods, a warrior riding in a car drawn by two he-goats amid thunder and lightning. Thor's Hammer, which had crushed the skull of many a Jutan, was said to have peculiar powers: when thrown it never failed to strike down the object at which it was aimed, and it always flew back to his hand.

In the early part of this century, the Kaiser had a crest with a German eagle holding a thunderbolt (Thor's Hammer) in its claw. In contrast to a right-handed Swastika, traditionally looked upon as an object of good fortune, Hitler's badge and flag bore a left-handed Swastika, viewed by occultists as equivalent to a reversed crucifix or saying the Lord's Prayer backwards. It was an omen of evil.

Heine, the great German Jewish poet whose books Hitler banned, gave a prophecy in 1834:

> Christianity has occasionally calmed the
> brutal German lust for battle, but cannot

70 The Cross and The Swastika

> destroy that savage joy. And when once that restraining talisman the Cross is broken, the old stone gods will rise from unremembered ruins and Thor will leap to life again and bring down his gigantic Hammer upon the Gothic cathedrals.

Under his evil banner, Hitler wielded the Hammer of Thor, which struck down with incredible accuracy every object at which it aimed, spreading its curse over occupied Europe.

Some writers have described the Fylfot as being composed of four gammas joined at the centre in the form of a boomerang. When thrown it ascends slowly into the air, whirling round and round until it reaches a considerable height and then returns, sweeping over the head of the thrower to strike the ground or an object behind him. It is worthy of note that the word 'Nazi' is practically the same as the Hebrew verb 'to startle', which is exactly what Hitler's Swastika did to the world until it finally returned as a 'hammer of indignation', smashing him down.

The Swastika is an emblem of delusion and degeneration whereas the cross of Jesus Christ, which Henry Gerecke was seeking to present to the prisoners, is a symbol of hope and life, the focal point of history and human experience.

In addition, Hitler and Hess were fascinated by astrology. Hitler soon became obsessed by the subject, and came to rely on the irrational and illogical. It is interesting to note that his horoscope for May 10th, 1940, the day on which he invaded Belgium and Holland, promised a successful outcome to any project undertaken.

Astrology must be distinguished from astronomy, the scientific and legitimate study of the stars. Astrology claims that the stars have an influence upon human affairs, and began about five thousand years ago when people worshipped the sun, the moon and other planets. They saw them as the owners of the heavens, each dwelling in his own house. Later development of this idea established the 'zodiac', an imaginary belt of the heavens outside which the sun, moon and major planets did not pass. Divided crosswise into twelve equal areas called 'signs of the zodiac', these became twelve 'houses'. Representing night and day, sun and moon were allocated one house each. The remaining ten houses were occupied by Venus, Saturn, Mars, Jupiter and Mercury.

The so-called 'Science of Astrology' flourished until late in the eighteenth century. It was little practised over the next hundred years until its revival in France and Britain at the close of the nineteenth century and in Germany about 1920.

All superstitious and occult practices breed harmful results, moulding the personality, stupifying the will and opening the mind to evil influences. Predictions often come true because of the power of auto-suggestion.

Hess became an astrological slave, despair and disorder assuming control of his life. While in Nuremberg he told the prison psychiatrist, Dr Kelly, that in late 1940 an astrologer he had consulted told him he was destined to bring the world a new order of peace. Later his old friend Professor Karl Haushofer, head of the Institute of Geopolitics in Munich, had a dream of Hess 'striding through the tapestried halls of English castles, bringing peace between the two great Nordic nations'.

On May 10th, 1941, Hess made his epic flight to

72 The Cross and The Swastika

Scotland in a stolen Messerschmmitt. His action, it would seem, was based on astrology. It is noteworthy that four months beforehand Dr. Schulte-Strathaus, a member of his staff and an occultist, had advised him of the astrological significance of an astronomical event to take place in the constellation of Taurus on that date.

May 10th was also twelve months exactly from the day when Hitler had launched his successful offensive upon Holland and Belgium. Perhaps, in his confused state of mind at that time, Hess set off as an instrument of peace, hoping to repeat Hitler's triumphs of the year before, even though some astrologers were beginning to doubt Hitler's ultimate success. It was as if he wished to put back the clock one year and make this special date bring a successful conclusion to his mission.

On May 14th, 1941, the Nazi Party newspaper *Volkischer Beobachter* reported:

> As was well known in Party circles, Rudolf Hess was in poor health for many years, and lately has had increasing resort to hypnotists, astrologers and so on. The extent to which these people are responsible for the mental confusion which led him to take his present step has still to be clarified.

On the same day the *The Times* of London published a report sent in by the paper's Swiss correspondent:

> Certain of Hess's closest friends have thrown an interesting light upon the affair. They say that Hess has always been Hitler's astrologer in secret. Up to

> last March he had always predicted
> good fortune and had always been right.
> Since then, notwithstanding the victories
> Germany has won, he had declared that
> the stars show that Hitler's meteoric
> career is approaching its climax.

Hess's departure angered Hitler, and he subsequently had astrologers and fortune-tellers arrested by the Gestapo. These included Dr Schulte-Strathaus and Karl Haushofer's son Albrecht, who was a friend of Hess. He was one of a number of occultists not in full sympathy with Nazi policies, and was in fact executed early in 1945 for his part in the bomb plot of July 20th, 1944 on Hitler's life.

Truly Henry Gerecke was fighting a battle between evil and good, between darkness and light. It is significant that both Hess and Rosenberg, with his new 'religion' of National Socialism, remained averse to any form of Christian counselling, notwithstanding Gerecke's faithfulness in visiting them on average four times each week through the trial months.

Eleven

Stille Nacht

The way of salvation begins when a sinner realises his lostness and his need of God's forgiveness. There is no other starting point. Murder, stealing, lying - all these sins and more will God forgive. But there is one sin He cannot: the unconfessed sin.

Gerecke sensed that Fritz Sauckel's confession of his sins, which were many, echoed the agony of a repentant soul. There was nothing he could do now by way of restitution to alleviate the hardships and sufferings caused through his programme of slavery which involved men, women and children taken from their homes. Nevertheless, God in His mercy had brought unmerited forgiveness into Sauckel's life and he was a different man. He confessed Jesus Christ as Saviour and was the first of the prisoners to express a desire for Holy Communion. Gratefully he accepted a Bible and a copy of Luther's Catechism in preparation for Gerecke's visits and instruction.

The men who sat with Jesus Christ at the table on the night of His betrayal, receiving from His hands bread and wine, heard Him say: 'This do in remembrance of Me.' Now nearly two thousand years later in a sparse cell in Nuremberg Prison two men knelt down in obedience to the Lord's command.

Turning to Sauckel, the chaplain asked:

'Do you believe that you are a sinner?'

'Yes, I believe it; I am a sinner,' Sauckel replied.
'How do you know this?'
'From the Ten Commandments; these I have not kept.'
'Are you sorry for your sins?'
'Yes, I am sorry that I have sinned against God.'
'What have you deserved of God by your sins?'
'His wrath and displeasure, temporal death and eternal damnation.'
'Do you also hope to be saved?'
'Yes, such is my hope.'
'In whom do you trust?'
'In my dear Lord Jesus Christ.'
'What then, has Christ done for you that you trust in Him?'
'He died for me and shed His blood for me on the cross for the forgiveness of sins.'

Court Sessions were held between 10am - 1pm and 2pm - 5pm. Gerecke resolved he must use every means and opportunity to win these men to Christ and his first priority was to get to know them better. Accordingly, he visited some early in the morning and others after their evening meal. During the day he spent several hours in court watching over his flock, listening to experienced prosecutors build up their case which inevitably would result in death sentences for some, perhaps all.

On November 29th, a documentary film on Nazi concentration camps, which had been found by American soldiers, was shown in the courtroom. Horrific scenes of tractors clearing away thousands of corpses - walking skeletons - Buchenwald crematorium - lampshades made from human skin - shocked the court. The prisoners reacted too! Göring and Hess turned their heads away from the screen and most turned to each other muttering, 'I don't believe it'. Fritzsche broke down and wept. Only Speer appeared to offer any resemblance of composure. From that time onwards the defence lawyers knew as never before, how difficult was their professional task.

As Christmas approached, Gerecke noticed a marked change in the attitude of Fritzsche, von Schirach and Speer. Sunday chapel services were providing a basis for conversation and enquiry each time he visited. Fritzsche, a soft spoken man, told Gerecke he was deeply ashamed of having turned against the church and hoped to come all the way back to Christ. Under the guidance of the chaplain he began reading set portions of Scripture and eagerly receiving instruction in Luther's Catechism. Von Schirach and Speer requested Bibles and Catechisms asking Gerecke, whom they now looked upon as a friend, to help them in their spiritual quest.

Most of the men had never attended a Christmas Eve service and for some it would be their last as well as their first. Gerecke recalled:

> The silence in the big prison was so profound that it hurt. All thirteen of my congregation were glad, I think, to come to chapel.

Carol followed carol and from his front seat which he occupied as religiously as those who once paid pew rent, Göring sang loudly. Intently, the men listened to Gerecke read Luke Chapter 2 and explain why God in His love sent Jesus into the world. There was infinite delight in the chaplain's heart in being able to say what he felt with conviction, coupled with love for the souls of his congregation. So much so that when he had finished Fritz Sauckel stood to his feet and said:

'We never took time to appreciate Christmas in its Biblical meaning. Tonight we are stripped of all material gifts and away from our people. But we have the Christmas story. And that's all we really need, isn't it?'

At the organ former SS Colonel Schellenberg, whom Gerecke had led to Christ, glided softly into 'Stille Nacht'. The men began humming, and a few quietly sang. Gerecke closed the service with prayer but no one moved and for five minutes or more they sat in silence. Each man was alone with his thoughts.

Gerecke wrote:

> On the way out, I wished them the peace of Christmas. Even the guards seemed less grim.

Christmas presents for the prisoners were forbidden due to orders issued by Colonel Andrus, notwithstanding pressures upon him to be more compassionate. A man of incomparable tenacity, he had banned gift packages for the prisoners in the wake of continual discoveries of hidden suicide kits. Outside the people of Nuremberg were starving and Andrus thought the prisoners' Christmas dinner consisting of soup, hash, potatoes, cabbage and coffee was reasonable fare.

Foremost in the men's minds was the whereabouts of their families. Unknown to them Colonel Andrus was making strenuous efforts to trace their location. Seven times he sent Gerecke to the airport to meet Raeder's wife, whom the Russians were holding but had promised to release. Each time Gerecke returned alone. The Russians were 'cold and heartless', remarked Raeder. Through their defence counsellors, Göring, Keitel, Schirach and Schacht had been told their wives were prisoners of the Americans but there were doubts about their children being with them. When Gerecke told Göring, he snapped, 'They're just like the Gestapo'. Hess never asked about his wife or her situation.

With the exception of Hess and Rosenberg all the men gladly accepted Gerecke's invitation to a Christmas Day service in the small chapel and again he joyfully presented Jesus Christ as a friend to the friendless and strength to the helpless, urging His claims upon their lives.

That night Henry Gerecke knelt down to speak with his friend - Jesus Christ. After several years away from home, he too felt lonely.

Twelve

Darkness and Light

Winter months exacted new inconveniences for Hitler's fallen heroes housed in spartan cells without heating. But Colonel Andrus couldn't relax his rules, looking upon each prisoner as a potential candidate for suicide.

During sleeping hours the cell lights were dimmed sufficiently to allow sleep but bright enough for the cell guard to see the prisoner at all times. A prisoner's head and hands were to remain visible whilst in bed; frequently, anxious guards disturbed any prisoner who unconsciously snuggled under the blankets for added comfort and warmth.

Meanwhile Fritzsche, von Schirach and Speer were seriously engaged in Bible study under the chaplain's direction as he endeavoured to make great Christian words such as grace, salvation, justification and faith intelligible to leading perpetrators of Nazism's hateful creed which had swept the helpless aside.

Hitler saw Christianity and Freemasonry as the major alternatives to National Socialism. 'One is either a German or a Christian. You cannot be both,' he said. In 1940 a Church of England Bishop remarked: 'There are no Christians among any of the German airmen captured in this country.' Prisoners were asked to state their religion and fifty per cent answered 'Nature', forty per cent replied 'Hitler' and ten per cent said they were atheists. It is interesting to note that 'Nature' indicated a worship of ancient Teuton gods.

Field Marshal Keitel was next to celebrate Holy Communion. With Gerecke's help he had read and memorised numerous verses of Scripture which spoke of God's mercy to sinners.

> He made a fine choice of Bible readings, hymns and prayers and read them himself, aloud. He was unashamed to kneel at his bed and together with me make confession of his sins. On his knees and under deep emotional stress, he received the Body and Blood of our Saviour in the bread and wine. With tears in his voice he said, 'You have helped me more then you know. May Christ, my Saviour, stand by me all the way. I shall need Him so much'.

The wonder of God's grace and forgiveness places it beyond a man-made system or catalogue of rules. The Bible, together with contemporary history, illustrates that no two people come to Christ in the same way. Jesus came to restore to mankind all that had been lost through sin. The world thought it had killed Jesus off but soon discovered that His resurrection power had transmitted itself through His disciples. Now, in the strangest of settings, Henry Gerecke was witnessing the living Christ move in the hearts of his 'congregation'.

Ribbentrop remained friendly so long as Gerecke stayed off the subject of Christ's salvation but Göring in his usual expansive style was mostly ready for Gerecke's visits with questions. He agreed that he might find some answers if he began reading the Bible! But first of all he wanted to be sure what Gerecke meant by 'inspiration' and why he called the Bible the 'Word of God'. In a reflective mood he listened to the chaplain's explanation:

'Holy men of God wrote the Bible. The prophets wrote the books of the Old Testament and the evangelists and the apostles wrote the books of the New Testament.'

Opening the Bible he read from 2 Peter chapter 1 verse 21:

> Holy men of God spake as they were
> moved by the Holy Ghost.

'This means that God the Holy Ghost moved the holy men to write, and put into their minds the very thoughts which they expressed and the very words which they wrote.'

Göring shook his head in disbelief, ridiculing the whole concept of 'inspiration' but said he would study further and make up his own mind on the matter.

Gerecke prepared the chapel, situated on the second floor of the prison block, for his three new communicants:

> It touched my heart to see the three big
> men on their knees about to receive the
> Lord's Supper. I felt sure others' prayers
> were with me because it was not
> possible to win them to the foot of the
> Cross without the intercessions of God's
> people. I am convinced God worked a
> change in their hearts through the Word
> that had been read and preached to
> them, and they were ready as every
> penitent is to ask God's forgiveness of

sins for Jesus' sake.

In turn, Gerecke asked the three men:
'I now ask you before God, is this your sincere confession, that you heartily repent of your sins, believe on Jesus Christ, and sincerely and earnestly purpose, by the assistance of God the Holy Ghost, henceforth to amend your sinful life? Then declare so by saying yes.'

With delight in his heart the chaplain gave bread and wine to Fritzsche, von Schirach and Speer.

> I shall never forget the sight of those three big men kneeling, asking that their sins be forgiven. So convincing was their bearing that the guards said to me, 'Chaplain, you'll not need us. This is holy business.' And they walked out.

In later talks with Albert Speer, Gerecke recalled:

> Frankly admitting the guilt of the Nazi regime, he told me he felt that the neglect of genuine Christianity caused its downfall.

Von Schirach was one of several prisoners who refused their evening meal following November's atrocity film shown in the courtroom.

> I had many talks with von Schirach, the Hitler Youth Leader. His mother was American born from Philadelphia. He had been confirmed at the age of fourteen but soon afterward became interested in the Nazi Youth movement.

> He became a leader in it before he was twenty. Now he realised, he said, that every energy should have been used to develop loyalty to Christian principles. On the witness stand he called Hitler the mass murderer of all history. Göring could have choked him for saying it.

At first, Grand Admiral Erich Raeder seemed enthusiastic over the chaplain's visits, feeling helped as he read and prayed with him. But when he was confronted with the matter of personal salvation, he raised many arguments:

> He seemed to be digging for justification of his own doubts. But quite the opposite has taken place and he was deeply interested in learning more. He would read the Scriptures for the coming Sunday's sermon and have questions ready when I visited again.

In the spring of 1946, Raeder opened his heart to the Lord Jesus Christ, accepting Him as Saviour. He struck up a friendship with von Schirach, sending letters to his cell asking an opinion on various portions of Scripture and their meaning. Later, after preparation, he joined Sauckel, Keitel, Fritzsche, von Schirach and Speer at the Communion Service.

Hjalmar Schacht rarely missed chapel services and regularly read the Bible provided by Gerecke, who was satisfied he had made his peace with God:

> He was very bitter about spending time in prison with men like Göring, who had

once jailed him. He refused communion
because, he said, his bitterness made
him spiritually unprepared for it. 'If this
is a fair trial, I'll be freed,' he declared,
'and then I should like to go to church
with my wife and partake of the Lord's
Supper.'

Baron von Neurath was one of the few prisoners who were smartly dressed. When he served as the German Ambassador to London he made many friends in Britain and had the Coronation of Edward VIII taken place he was the British Government's choice as German representative. During the first few months of confinement his record at chapel services was irregular. Gerecke found him difficult to communicate with... and a challenge!

He was witnessing miracles in the hearts of men whose Third Reich had rained upon mankind bestialities hitherto unknown. Henry Gerecke prayed that aristocrat von Neurath, whom Hitler used to make Nazism respectable, would identify himself with the Christ of Calvary who alone could save him from sin and hell. Faithfully, he reviewed the Apostles' Creed according to Luther's Catechism in the hope that von Neurath would see himself in the light of God's Word:

> Being born again, not of corruptible seed,
> but of incorruptible, by the Word of God,
> which liveth and abideth forever.
> 1 Peter 1:23.

Henry Gerecke was a wise counsellor who prayed each step of the way and had an implicit trust in the Scriptures. Von Neurath read:

> By grace are ye saved, through faith, and
> that not of yourselves; it is the gift of
> God; not of works, lest any man should
> boast.
>
> Eph. 2: 8,9.

He saw that being born again was altogether a work of the Holy Spirit involving a personal repentance of the sins which separated him from God; that Christ had paid the penalty of sin and it was up to him to ask forgiveness and by faith receive Christ into his life. Gerecke recalled, 'As we went along, he manifested genuine interest.' This led to a crisis experience when the old Baron admitted his need of salvation.

> His family was very gratified at his
> religious progress and wrote to me often
> about his 'getting right with God'.

Grand Admiral Dönitz challenged Gerecke to 'show us what you are preaching about', which was a constant reminder that despite all his ears heard in court he must distinguish between a man's sins and the man himself. Any betrayal of Christian love would instantly negate all his labours and make him a barrier to the prisoners' salvation. More than any of them realised, Henry Gerecke had to keep his soul sweet and in tune with his Lord.

> We grieved at our failures with the men,
> rejoiced at each slight indication of
> spiritual awakening.

Dr Funk, the Reichsbank president who succeeded Schacht, told Gerecke: 'Every German has a moral guilt

88 The Cross and The Swastika

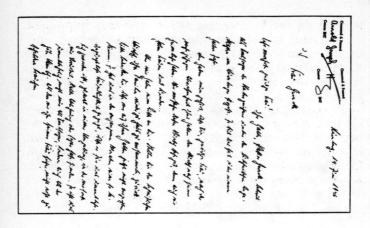

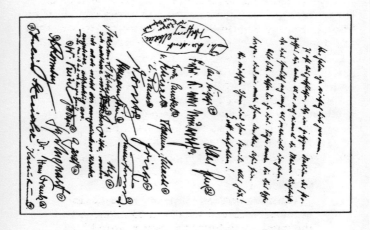

Letter to Henry Gerecke's wife from the prisoners

in starting the war and in the things that happened during the war.' It was proven by witnesses and documentary evidence that the vaults of his bank contained gold from teeth of concentration camp victims. Funk denied any knowledge of this, but said he was guilty because he was ultimately responsible. However, his honesty did not stretch far enough to acknowledge his own sins and need of salvation. Wilhelm Frick, an eager Nazi, regular at the chapel services, showed an interest in the Gospel but his legalistic attitude kept Gerecke at a safe distance and he was never really sure what was going on in his heart.

* * * *

In May, 1946, rumours began to circulate that older officers of the United States personnel would soon be allowed to return home if they chose to do so. That would include Gerecke, the defendants reasoned:

> I was fifty four at the time. When they moaned over separation from their families, I had done a little mild griping of my own. I probably mentioned my wife's health and the fact that I had not seen her for two and a half years. At any rate they decided that Mrs Gerecke would be the chief influence for my return home.
>
> Consequently, my wife back in Missouri received what someone termed the most incredible letter ever sorted by St Louis postal clerks. It was written in almost illegible German script.

The Cross and The Swastika

Composed by Hans Fritsche the letter read:

> Your husband has been taking religious care of the undersigned for more than half a year. We have now heard that you wish to see him back home after his absence of several years. Because we also have wives and children we understand this wish of yours well. Nevertheless we are asking you to put off your wish to gather your family around you. Please consider that we cannot miss your husband now. During the past months he has shown us uncompromising friendliness of such a kind that we cannot be without him in these surroundings in which - but for him - we find only prejudice, cold disdain or hatred. It is impossible for any other to break through the walls that have been built up around us, in a spiritual sense even stronger than a material one. We have simply come to love him.
>
> Please leave him with us. Certainly you will feel this sacrifice and we shall be deeply indebted to you. We send our best wishes to you and your family. God be with you.

Sent through the regular prison censorship, the letter bore the signatures of all defendants including those of Hess and Rosenberg and the six Catholic prisoners under the care of Chaplain Sixtus O'Connor. Although Gerecke had no direct responsibility for the Roman

Catholics he had made regular courtesy calls to their cells. Colonel General Jodl added a note: 'I readily add my name to this appeal, even though I do not belong to the Evangelical Lutheran Church.' Former diplomat Franz von Papen wrote: 'So do I, from the bottom of my heart.'

Immediately Mrs Alma Gerecke, surprised by the galaxy of signatories, yet greatly moved with the realisation of the extent to which God was using her husband, sent a cable: 'Please stay on... they need you!'

Her husband too was moved:

> Hitler's strong boys who had scourged Christianity and broken the Ten Commandments more than any other scoundrels in history were beseeching an American housewife...

JUDGMENT

I kneel by my bed and look up to heaven and ask God to open my daddy's heart and let Jesus in.

Edda Göring

Thirteen

Judgment Day

The long trial ended on August 31st, 1946 and the eight judges went into secret session to consider their verdicts. Having little else to do the defendants were permitted to take their daily walks in a yard at one side of the cell block.

Cell searches increased to sometimes as many as four per week. Colonel Andrus was nervous, having been informed that Judgment Day might not be announced until late September. On entering a cell, guards ordered each prisoner to strip and stand in a corner whilst they thoroughly searched his bedding, clothing and every personal item.

Gerecke saw how depressed the men had become and asked Colonel Andrus if he could hold chapel services each evening after supper. At the same time both chaplains petitioned the International Military Tribunal to allow the prisoners' families to visit them. Justice Lawrence, president of the tribunal, replied: 'Have them come before the verdict'.

Often the prisoners' children stayed in Gerecke's office on visiting days:

> When the Schacht children, aged three and five years, were there, we really had our hands full. They were the Katzenjammer Kids in action, thinking

up all sorts of pranks to disturb the sombre prison atmosphere. I remember Frau Sauckel, mother of those eleven children, as simple and kind.

Emmy Göring was a woman of considerable grace and charm. With tears in her eyes she urged her daughter Edda to talk to me. I asked the little girl if she said her prayers.

She replied, 'I pray every night.'

'And how do you pray?' I enquired.

'I kneel by my bed and look up to heaven and ask God to open my daddy's heart and let Jesus in.'

When I tried to talk in a similar vein with Alfred Rosenberg's daughter, a pretty thirteen year old, she interrupted, 'Don't give me any of that prayer stuff.'

I asked, 'Is there anything at all I can do for you?'

'Yes,' she answered. 'Got a cigarette?'

The special room arranged for visitors was anything but private. Two guards stood by each prisoner and on the visitors' side, separated by a high glass screen to prevent the couples touching each other, one of the chaplains and another officer were in attendance.

During these visits, the little ones became very dear to us. It was my privilege and delight to speak to some of them about the Saviour. Our hearts were heavy as we bid these families farewell at the end of their visits.

Time was short! Once Judgment Day was declared Gerecke was not sure how soon executions would take place. As he gathered his little congregation together each evening he preached with intensity, praying that God would yet touch further hearts with the power of the Gospel of the Lord Jesus Christ. 'It was gratifying to see the working of the Holy Spirit on some of these men,' he wrote.

For nearly a year von Ribbentrop had heard the chaplain proclaim Christ as the answer, talking of the Cross and the power of the Blood of Jesus and explaining that faith is simply the channel through which God's grace is received. Ribbentrop could hold out no longer, seeking God's forgiveness and opening his heart to Christ:

> One of my most heartening experiences was observing the slow and steady progress of Joachim von Ribbentrop, the diplomat, from cool indifference to a truly sincere Christian faith.

This upset Frau Ribbentrop, and Gerecke wrote:

> She certainly made it as difficult for me as she could through her letters - she wrote that she would offset my influence on her husband in every way she could.

On September 30th, the day which the world had eagerly awaited, came the judgment, a lengthy pronouncement read in turn by each of the judges in his own language. Mr Justice Jackson for the United States said:

98 The Cross and The Swastika

Defendants in court

> No half century ever witnessed slaughter on such a scale, such cruelties and inhumanities, such wholesale deportation of people into slavery, such annihilation of minorities ... These men in this dock on the face of this record, were not strangers to this programme of crime, nor was their connection with it remote or obscure. They are the very highest serving authorities in their respective fields and in the Nazi State. No one lives who, at least until the very last moments of the war, outranked Göring in position, power and influence. No soldier stood above Keitel or Jodl, and no sailor above Raeder or Dönitz. Who can be responsible for the double-faced diplomacy if not Foreign Ministers von Neurath and Ribbentrop and the diplomatic handyman, von Papen? ... If you come to say of these men that they are not guilty, it would be as true to say that there has been no war, there are no slain, there has been no crime.

Next day, October 1st, each of the defendants in turn stood alone in the dock. Göring stood first to be told that his sentence was death by hanging. For a moment he remained quite still, his face drawn and pale, then walked out of the courtroom to be accompanied back to his cell. In the hushed courtroom Gerecke watched his congregation receive their sentences, some bravely but most in a state of shock.

The four counts of indictment were:

1. Conspiracy to commit crimes alleged in other courts.
2. Crimes against peace.
3. War crimes.
4. Crimes against humanity.

DEATH SENTENCES were given to:

Göring:	Guilty on all four counts
Ribbentrop:	Guilty on all four counts
Keitel:	Guilty on all four counts
Frick:	Guilty on counts two, three and four
Sauckel:	Guilty on counts three and four
Rosenberg:	Guilty on all four counts

SENTENCES OF LIFE IMPRISONMENT were given to:

Hess:	Guilty on counts one and two
Raeder:	Guilty on counts one two and three
Funk:	Guilty on counts two, three and four

LONG PRISON SENTENCES were given to:

Von Schirach:	(20 years) Guilty on count four
Speer:	(20 years) Guilty on counts three and four.
Von Neurath:	(15 years) Guilty on all four counts

Dönitz: (10 years) Guilty on counts two and three

NOT GUILTY
Fritzsche and Schacht

Chaplain Sixtus O'Connor's men received:

DEATH SENTENCES

Kaltenbrunner: Guilty on counts three and four
Frank: Guilty on counts three and four
Seyss-Inquart: Guilty on counts two, three and four
Streicher: Guilty on count four
Jodl: Guilty on all four counts

NOT GUILTY
Von Papen

For security reasons, prison chapel services were brought to an end, the chaplains spending most of their time visiting men in 'death row' as it was called. Other prisoners had been moved to second tier cells.

The work became increasingly difficult because 'Stars and Stripes' had announced that the condemned men would be hanged fifteen days after 'Judgment Day'.

Their attorneys had read this item with a great deal of interest and had conveyed the thought to their clients during the few meetings they still had with their men. Every man on 'death row' seemed quite certain that the executions would take place on October 16th and every man wanted to know which part of the day they would go into eternity. Would it be in the morning? Would it be at noontime?

By permission of the four prosecuting nations those in 'death row' were allowed one last opportunity to speak to their wives:

> They were difficult hours for the convicted and their loved ones, myself and Chaplain O'Connor. Keitel did not want to see his wife because, as he said, 'I am too emotionally unstrung and I simply couldn't bear up under it.'
>
> I heard Ribbentrop plead with his wife that their children be kept in the church and be brought up in the fear and admonition of the Lord. This statement coming from Ribbentrop is especially interesting to me because at the beginning of my work I discovered that the whole family had withdrawn from the church. Perhaps uncharitably, I labelled Frau von Ribbentrop the most ungodly woman I ever met. I heard her husband plead with her, 'Have the children baptised, sweetheart.' Finally, she gave in and I helped her arrange for the baptism of their two boys at a neighbouring church.
>
> Frau Sauckel promised her husband that the children should stay close to the Cross of Jesus Christ.
>
> Göring asked his wife what their little daughter Edda had said about the whole situation. She replied that Edda had said

she wanted to meet her daddy in
Heaven. He stood up and turned away.
For the first time I saw tears in his eyes.

Of all the prisoners, Hermann Göring seemed to trouble Gerecke the most.

Fourteen

Tussle with the Big Man

Each night, Schellenberg played hymns on the chapel organ which the men found soothing as they lay listening on their cots. Gerecke knew as he made his evening visits that it would be the last earthly music eleven of them would hear. In a few hours time they would be put to death and although under orders not to divulge the exact day and hour the prisoners themselves eased his strain in carrying such an awesome secret. Somehow they knew it would be within the next twelve hours.

Field Marshal Keitel was reading his Bible when Gerecke entered to share a devotional session; as usual Keitel turned to the Scriptures heralding the power of the Blood of the Lord Jesus Christ, ending his prayer, 'God be merciful to me a sinner'. Sensing his appointment with the executioner was near, he requested Gerecke to have him buried in a cemetery lot near a family chapel.

Praying with Ribbentrop was now a delight. He was so honest in testifying to the assurance in his heart of Christ's salvation. In a matter of weeks he had read much of the Bible and the Catechism and was ready to take communion. Unable to use the chapel, Gerecke knelt down with him beside his cot, a hallowed spot, and gave him bread and wine.

Around 8.30pm he greeted Hermann Göring who had

told him after his wife had visited for the last time: 'When I left my wife ... I died.' A connoisseur of paintings, works of art and literature, Göring epitomised the early German princes. Delighting in pomp and colourful military ceremony his magnificent wardrobe of uniforms ensured that he was well dressed for each occasion. Yet, like the princes who loved beauty, he could administer cruelties, engaging in murder and violence.

The former Reichsmarschall accepted Gerecke's handwritten devotion, the product of considerable preparation, promising to read it, but he persistently interrupted their conversation with his guesswork as to when the executions would take place. More than the others he quizzed Gerecke, hoping he would confirm his supposition by stating the precise time:

> I tried to keep him on the subject of eternal values and how a man can be prepared to die and to meet his God. In the course of our conversation I found him making sport of the Bible account of the creation of man. He ridiculed the idea of the Divine inspiration of the Scriptures and refused to accept the great fundamental doctrine of the Gospel that Jesus died for every sinner. There was an outright denial of the power of the Cross and the meaning of that Holy Innocent Blood that was shed upon the Cross for salvation of sinners. He said he thought that when he was dead that was the end of everything.

Approximately seventy chapel services had been held

and Göring had attended them all. He had heard preaching based upon the Word of God which knows our nature, our habits, our whole constitution, and that can immediately address itself to our personal necessities! But he had hardened his heart, a deflating experience for Gerecke who knew that when next he called upon him it would be to accompany the Reichsmarschall to the gallows and there would be little time for conversation. Once Göring had remarked, 'You don't start a war unless you can finish it', a remark Gerecke applied to his present situation as he battled for this man's soul:

> He put one question that evening which surprised me a great deal. 'Pastor,' he said, 'how do you celebrate the Lord's Supper?'

After he had categorically denied so much the question was unexpected, but it was asked sincerely. Henry Gerecke was a man of spiritual perception, discerning the work of the Holy Spirit and striving to bring the big man to a place of brokenness before the Lord. Opening his Bible he read relevant portions of Scripture, relating them to Luther's Catechism containing direct questions for those intending to take communion:

'You see!' he said. 'Only fully surrendered and penitent Christians should partake of the Lord's Supper.'

Angrily, Göring argued that no German pastor would have dared to refuse him, concluding:

'I thought I would just ask in case there was anything in this Christianity business of yours.'

'I cannot with a clear conscience give you the Lord's Supper,' Gerecke answered, 'because you deny the very

108 The Cross and The Swastika

Christ who instituted it. You may be on a church roll, but you do not have faith in Christ and have not accepted Him as your Saviour, therefore you are not a Christian and as a Christian pastor I cannot commune you.'

Time was short. Soon Hermann Göring would have a rope around his neck and be ushered into a lost eternity, which grieved the St. Louis pastor, who pleaded with him to repent and turn to Christ:

> When I asked him to remember what his little daughter had said about wanting to meet him in heaven, he answered, 'She believes in your Saviour, but I'll take my chances.'

Gerecke knelt down, informing Göring he was going to pray for him. He remained sitting on his cot listening to the man of God pour out his soul in love, praying that Hermann Göring's eyes would be opened and his heart become receptive to the Christ who had died for him. Without speaking, Göring remained where he was for about two minutes after Gerecke had finished, looking downcast and depressed.

'Pastor,' he said as Gerecke was about to leave, 'I believe in God. I believe He watches over the affairs of men. But only the big ones. He is too great to bother about little matters like what becomes of Hermann Göring.'

At 10.45pm that same evening, Gerecke was in the guardroom chatting with a fellow officer. Suddenly, a distraught security guard burst in:

'Sir, Göring is having a fit,' he said.

Gerecke and the officer ran to his cell a hundred yards away:

> Göring was lying on his back with his left hand hanging over the side of his cot. Gurgling sounds came from his throat, his eyes rolling as I picked up his left hand and felt for a pulse ... there was none. 'Get the doctor,' I told the guard, 'this man is dying'. Desperately, not knowing what else to do, I leaned close to the unconscious man and spoke Scripture in his ear.

Dr Pluecker, the German prison medical practitioner, promptly arrived followed by his staff, an American doctor, then the officer of the guard. In a matter of less than one minute the tiny cell was full.

> The officer reached over and picked up the right hand which was lying clutched outside the blanket. There was a rustle and an envelope fell to the floor. The envelope was torn open at the top and bore the name of 'H. Göring'. It contained three notes in Göring's handwriting, one of which was addressed to the prison commandant. Enclosed in the envelope was a small brass container made from a standard German cartridge shell. Apparently, it had contained a vial of potassium cyanide which Göring contrived to crunch between his teeth without being observed.

The notes were delivered to the military committee but their contents have never been made known.

However, the Council's investigation report on the affair cleared all prison staff of responsibility or conspiracy.

Numerous theories have been offered as to how Göring obtained the poison but in spite of many opinions ranging from his wife slipping it to him during a visit to his defence counsel passing it whilst in court, hidden in papers, no explanation has satisfactorily withstood close scrutiny. If an outside body had been responsible, with the passing of years no doubt the person in question would have come forward.

Perhaps Gerecke's opinion, expressed at the time, is the true one. At one of the Sunday chapel services he had touched upon the sin of 'self-destruction'. A few days later Colonel Andrus had implemented new and stiffer security measures. Göring was the only prisoner to speak to Gerecke about the matter:

'What kind of foolishness is this?' Göring demanded. 'They ought to know it's impossible here for us to do anything against ourselves.'

Thinking over the whole affair, Gerecke felt this was a 'crocodile act', believing that Göring's suicide was planned well in advance and that he had managed with diabolical cleverness to conceal poison for use when the time came. This assumption he based in part on the air of secret triumph which Göring often wore:

> It was as if he were saying, 'Go ahead fellows: do with me what you like. I'll fix you in the end.' Self execution by potassium cyanide was his crowning achievement.

Major Fred Teich, assistant chief security officer, also believed he had carried the poison since the beginning of the trial, ruling out any possibility that it had been slipped to him. 'Security measures have been too stringent for that,' he said. In fact Göring had been searched one hundred times during his stay at Nuremberg and had had a vial of poison taken from a tin of powdered coffee in his possession shortly after his surrender.

One of the German defence lawyers, Dr Friedrich Bergold, recalled that towards the end of the trial after he had made his final plea for Martin Bormann who was tried 'in absentia', Göring called him to the prisoners' dock and, smirking and rubbing his hands together, said:

'Doctor, you were wonderful. I am so glad that you quoted the old German proverb to these people - 'The Nurembergers hang no one before they really have them.'

Now agitated by the heavy burden of delivering his charges to the executioner in two hours' time, Andrus asked the chaplain to inform the prisoners, who had been awakened by the commotion, that Göring was dead:

> Most of them thought it was pretty small of Mr Göring to get out of the situation in this manner. For over a year he had bragged about how brave he would be until the end. Now, several of them thought he had missed the chance to become a legend to the German people.

Henry Gerecke returned to his quarters to prepare himself for his greatest ordeal - the executions - saddened by his failure with Hermann Göring:

112 The Cross and The Swastika

If I blundered in my approach to reach this man's heart and soul with the meaning of the Cross of Jesus ... I hope a Christian world will forgive me.

Fifteen

Tode Durch den Strang

At 9pm on Tuesday October 16th, 1946 cell lights were dimmed and the prisoners settled in for the night. Colonel Andrus had decided not to tell the condemned that in three hours time they would be awakened and prepared for execution.

Five days previously, in great secrecy, a gallows had been erected in the prison gymnasium where some of them had taken evening walks as an alternative to using the exercise yard during inclement weather conditions. Apart from this the American guards had used it for basketball.

The noise outside Göring's cell had awakened the prisoners who were now trying to sleep again after the clatter had died down. At 11.45pm they were disturbed once again. Now at last they were informed they were about to die and told to dress. A short while later Colonel Andrus, accompanied by the Public Prosecutor and an interpreter, read the death sentence to each man, ending 'Tode durch den strang' ... death by the rope.

A last supper was offered - sausage and salad, fruit salad, and coffee - but few accepted.

Since Göring had committed suicide von Ribbentrop headed the list as first to die. Gerecke entered his cell at 1am, spending a few minutes with him in prayer.

> I heard him say that he put all his trust

> in the Blood of the Lamb that taketh away the sins of the world. While yet in his cell, he asked God to have mercy on his soul. Then the signal was given to start down the corridor towards the execution chamber.

Ribbentrop's hands were placed behind his back and handcuffed. Colonel Andrus led the procession followed by the two chaplains side by side and behind them Ribbentrop in between two guards. Across the yard in the gymnasium hangman John Woods, an American army sergeant who had already hanged three hundred and forty seven people, awaited them.

On a platform stood three gallows of thick unplaned wood and in a corner, draped in black cloth, lay eleven coffins. Ribbentrop, looking brave, climbed the thirteen steps and as he stood under the gallows his handcuffs were removed to be replaced by thin cords. His ankles were bound by a guard with an army webbing belt:

> There he stood face to face with the impassive spectators assembled as official witnesses. An American army officer asked if he had a last word to say. I don't recall all of von Ribbentrop's final statement but it ended with, 'God have mercy on my soul'. Then he turned to me and said - and my heart still warms when I think of it - 'I'll see you again.'
>
> I spoke a brief prayer. Then the big black hood was pulled over his face, the knot with thirteen coils adjusted behind his head - and he dropped through the trap door.

Returning to the prison corridor, the chaplains waited for the signal to come with the second man. This was Keitel, Chief of Staff of the Wehrmacht:

> Our period of prayer was drenched with tears. As we came to the execution chamber, Keitel's eyes took one swift glance at the first gallows. That look told me he knew his friend Ribbentrop was hanging there. We ascended the steps of the second gallows and repeated together a prayer we had both learned from our mothers. He then said, 'I thank you, and those who sent you, with all my heart.'

Next it was Chaplain O'Connor's turn to accompany one of his flock to the scaffold, scar-faced Kaltenbrunner. After giving his name he said, 'I have served my people and my Fatherland with a willing heart. I have done my duty in accordance with the laws of the Fatherland. I regret that crimes were committed in which I had no part.'

The third of Gerecke's 'congregation' to be led out was Fritz Sauckel:

> When the signal was given, my heart actually skipped a beat. He had been so unnerved during the final twenty four hours that I wondered if he would bear up. When he stood on the trap door and spoke of his wife and children, I was so jolted that I thought for a moment I could not go on. I, too, was becoming unnerved by that time. I managed to

> have a final prayer, after which he went
> quickly into eternity.

Colonel Andrus allowed Gerecke a few minutes in Frick's cell before he was escorted to the gallows. Although Frick had been regularly to chapel services and had accepted a Bible, Gerecke bemoaned his failure in getting close to him. The lack of intimacy relegated discussions on spiritual matters into an impersonal and shallow presentation of cold doctrine. Andrus waited outside as Gerecke had his final words with the man in the bright tweed jacket, who showed signs of exhaustion.

'I've got something to tell you,' said Frick. As the chaplain listened he rejoiced over another lost soul who had discovered the reality of Jesus Christ as Saviour, for Frick said that he believed that the Blood of Jesus had washed away his sins.

Last in Gerecke's group was Alfred Rosenberg, who had to the end refused all spiritual help.

> I asked if I might say a prayer for him.
> He smiled and said, 'No thank you'. He
> lived without a Saviour and that is the
> way he died.

The remaining four to be executed were all in the care of Chaplain Sixtus O'Connor. Jew-baiter Julius Streicher, like Hess and Rosenberg, refused the chaplain's offer of help. As he walked up the steps of the scaffold he shouted, 'Heil Hitler'. Turning in hangman Woods' direction he sniggered, 'The Bolsheviks will hang you one day'. Gerecke maintains that despite many press reports quoting what the condemned shouted after the hood was placed over their heads, Streicher was the only one to cry out, repeating his wife's name.

Frank, who had returned to the Roman Catholic Church and who satisfied O'Connor with a sincere repentance, thanked Colonel Andrus for all his kindness, saying from the scaffold: 'I pray to God to take my soul. May the Lord receive me mercifully.'

Jodl too had rejected O'Connor's help but died bravely as did the last man, Seyss-Inquart, who said:

'I hope this execution is the last act of the tragedy of the Second World War and that the lesson of this war will make for peace and understanding among the peoples. I believe in Germany.'

According to German law, next of kin had a right to collect bodies for burial but the Allies, fearing a future generation might venerate their resting places into shrines, loaded the coffins into two lorries and a little after 4am they left the prison under heavy guard heading for Dachau. The bodies were incinerated in the ovens of the former concentration camp and thus Gerecke was unable to carry out Keitel's last wishes to be buried near a church.

Henry Gerecke wanted to be alone, returning to the small chapel, its use now ended but the memories of which would forever live within his heart:

> Thus died eleven men of intelligence and ability who, differently influenced, could have been, I am convinced, a blessing to the world instead of a curse. For all my own blunderings and failures with them, I ask forgiveness.

EPILOGUE

Sixteen

The Man With a Warm Heart

Whilst sitting in Albert Speer's home in Heidelberg, Southern Germany, my first question to the tall, dignified former Reich Minister for Armaments and War Production caused an almost embarrassing silence as he stared into space. I looked to Frau Speer for comfort. He leaned further back into his chair, deep in thought and staring at the wall above my head: 'Henry Gerecke,' he said slowly with feeling, 'was a man with a warm heart ... he cared.'

As I listened to Speer I began to wish that I could have met Gerecke in the flesh. Speer spent twenty years in Spandau Prison, Berlin and during that time read and studied eighteen large volumes of theology. This was the fruit of Gerecke's ministry and his own desire for the truth of God's Word. He told me he couldn't explain the change which came into his life when he accepted Christ; many times he had tried to understand it. There was a church in the Bavarian mountains he retreated to for a brief spell away from home surroundings in order to pray and meditate. 'Without Pastor Gerecke,' he said, 'I could never have got through those days at Nuremberg.'

On October 11th 1961, fifteen years to the day after arriving in Nuremberg, Henry Gerecke died. He was chaplain to Illinois State Penitentiary at Menard and collapsed at the prison gates when on his way to take the prison Bible class. The prisoners took the news very badly and even the most hardened were shaken, requesting the Warden to let them see him just once more.

'They held him in high esteem,' Warden Ross Randolph said. 'He talked their language. They respected him. He never lost his temper with them but they knew they couldn't fool him.'

Warden Randolph got clearance from state officials for Gerecke's body to be taken to the prison. Former Illinois state auditor Orville Hodge, a confidant of the chaplain's, who was serving a fifteen year sentence for the theft of one and a half million dollars, announced over the prison loudspeaker system that all inmates except some in the psychiatric division would be permitted to view the body.

More than eight hundred convicts filed past the coffin. 'There were tears,' the Warden said. He also believed it was the first time in Illinois, and possibly in the nation, that arrangements had been made for prisoners to pay tribute to an individual in this way.

As a memorial to the man that many others found had 'a warm heart', one of the prison's chapels was named in his honour and the convicts raised a collection to help furnish a family prayer room in a new hospital.

I tried to continue Henry Gerecke's ministry by corresponding with Grand Admiral Karl Dönitz. The last letter I received from him was two months before his death on Christmas Eve, 1980. I sent him some Christian literature which I hope he read and applied to his life. My efforts to visit Rudolf Hess, who at the time of writing is still in Spandau Prison, have been blocked by the Russians.

Perhaps one last word from the far-sighted Henry Gerecke will be a warning to all of us:

A little group got into the saddle of governmental affairs. Little by little it got into full control. First it gained a foothold because it seemed to cater to the working classes. From talks with the defendants and many witnesses in the Nuremberg Prison, I have concluded that many who went along with the party thought it a good thing for their country. But 'Clique Control' began to grow. It took a toe-hold on the country through public works programmes. It did away with unemployment. The cost of living was low and men could support their families on small salaries.

But somewhere along the line this group got the idea of expansion through aggression and from that moment on plans got under way for war. All smaller groups, about twenty-nine parties, were swallowed up and there started a reign of persecution against all opposition. The clique saw an opportunity to do something that would pull others along. Many went along at the beginning, thinking they had found something good for the Fatherland.

Only a few got to the top, and they began to crack the whip over their people. Millions were caught in this political current. However, many saw trouble after the Anschluss of Austria. In one of their secret meetings Hitler told Raeder, 'You see, it worked. I told you so. The prayers of a thousand years have

> been answered.' Raeder concluded that nothing could stop Hitler from then on. The Clique was in the saddle and in control. Once on their books as a member, no matter how small and insignificant, you were stuck.
>
> Your convictions were stifled. It was dangerous to protest and you could not resign.
>
> Let us remember that the gross hates and cruelties which climaxed in the careers of the Nazi leaders had their inception in the petty hates, prejudices and compromises of millions of little men and women - some of them quite pious too.

Albert Speer told me that from the day of his release from Spandau, men with political 'squints' had endeavoured to involve him in bizarre movements. 'But I've learned the lessons of history,' he said.

The Greatest Trial in History will ever be a talking point. Today, there is a strong voice propagating its illegality in international law. But the fact is that it did take place. The arguments will continue and new stories come to light. Who knows? Perhaps Hermann Göring did hear the Scriptures Henry Gerecke spoke in his ear as he was dying, and repented.

When Gerecke first went to Nuremberg, he had prayed for the ability to love 'Hitler's Gang', the most hated men of their time. Throughout the months, he had spoken to them faithfully of Jesus Christ, their only hope of eternal forgiveness, and had seen the power of God at work in men's hearts. Truly, he could hear and apply the

The Man With a Warm Heart 125

Saviour's words:

> Rejoice with Me; for I have found My sheep which was lost. I say unto you, that likewise joy shall be in heaven over one sinner that repenteth, more then over ninety and nine just persons, which need no repentance.